PEOPLE YOU SHOULD KNOW

TOP 101 WORLD LEADERS

Edited by Jeanne Nagle

Britannica®
Educational Publishing

IN ASSOCIATION WITH

ROSEN
EDUCATIONAL SERVICES

Published in 2014 by Britannica Educational Publishing (a trademark of Encyclopædia Britannica, Inc.) in association with The Rosen Publishing Group, Inc.
29 East 21st Street, New York, NY 10010

Distributed exclusively by Rosen Publishing.
To see additional Britannica Educational Publishing titles, go to rosenpublishing.com

First Edition

Britannica Educational Publishing
J.E. Luebering: Director, Core Reference Group
Anthony L. Green: Editor, Compton's by Britannica

Rosen Publishing
Hope Lourie Killcoyne: Executive Editor
Jeanne Nagle: Editor
Nelson Sá: Art Director
Brian Garvey: Designer, Cover Design
Cindy Reiman: Photography Manager

Library of Congress Cataloging-in-Publication Data

Top 101 world leaders/editor, Jeanne Nagle. — First edition.
    pages cm. — (People you should know)
Includes bibliographical references and index.
ISBN 978-1-62275-124-2 (library binding)
1. Heads of state—Biography—Juvenile literature. 2. Statesmen—Biography—Juvenile literature. I. Nagle, Jeanne. II. Title: Top one hundred one world leaders.
D107.T67 2014
352.23092'2—dc23
[B]
                                                                2013033316

Manufactured in the United States of America

On the cover: Pictured are (top, left to right) Abraham Lincoln *thatsmymop/ Shutterstock.com*; the Dalai Lama *ocphoto/Shutterstock.com*; Margaret Thatcher *WPA Pool/Getty Images*; Mohandas Gandhi *Elliot & Fry/Hulton Archive/Getty Images*; (bottom, left to right) Joan of Arc *Renata Sedmakova/Shutterstock.com*; Winston Churchill *Michael Ochs Archives/Getty Images*; Queen Victoria *Abraham Badenhorst/ Shutterstock.com*; and Cleopatra *Time & Life Pictures/Getty Images*.

Cover and interior pages (top) © *iStockphoto.com/René Mansi*

CONTENTS

YA923
TOP

5

18

43

56

79

99

INTRODUCTION

I f history is any indication, most of today's important political and governmental leaders in our world today will largely be forgotten in a decade or two. Over time, the contributions of many world leaders begin to fade in importance as new ideas and individuals capture the public's attention. However, the reputations of a select few will not only endure beyond their lifetimes but will start to grow in importance, gaining recognition far beyond their time and place. *People You Should Know: Top 101 World Leaders* is a collection of biographies of many of the latter group.

There are two defining characteristics of great leaders. First, they have been people of action whose fame, ideas, and breadth of accomplishment endure over time. Victorious emperors such as Julius Caesar of Rome and Napoleon I of France typically exhibit these qualities, combining impressive military conquests with major social, economic, and political reforms. American President Abraham Lincoln and South African President Nelson Mandela are known for their civil rights accomplishments as well as for the wisdom and mercy that each used to heal and unify their divided nations. The world also pays attention to and admires leaders who succeed by overcoming great obstacles. Female leaders, such as England's Elizabeth I and Russia's Catherine the Great, had to tread carefully, based on their gender, but each significantly contributed to the progress and prosperity of their respective nations.

The second defining characteristic of world leaders is their ability to exert tremendous influence and inspire confidence and loyalty. Indeed, all great world leaders have attracted and maintained legions of disciples who believed in and promoted their ideas. Some, like Britain's Winston Churchill, connected to the people through soaring rhetoric—meaning he motivated and inspired people through exceptional public speaking—and devotion to duty. Others, such as China's Mao Zedong and Poland's Lech Wałęsa, attracted loyal followers by becoming the voice and champion of the common man.

Merely because a world leader possesses these traits does not mean his or her leadership has been good or beneficial for their societies.

Germany's Adolf Hitler, the Soviet Union's Joseph Stalin, and Cambodia's Pol Pot were skilled and seemingly popular leaders who inspired followers, but who were also guilty of committing great and terrible brutality against millions of their own citizens. Clearly, in cases such as these, "great" does not always mean "good." What it does mean is that these great leaders were so highly influential that they changed not only their own societies but left a lasting legacy that impacted the future of the entire world.

One way to judge who is or isn't a great leader is to use the historian's process. Historians first establish and analyze the verifiable facts. Next, they pay close attention to the motives, beliefs, goals, and values of both leaders and their followers. Finally, they evaluate leaders by the ethics and practices of their own place and time. The individuals profiled in these pages have been put to the test and been judged to be great world leaders.

MAHMOUD AHMADINEJAD

(b. 1956–)

D espite his service as mayor of the capital city of Tehran, Iranian Mahmoud Ahmadinejad was largely considered a political outsider when he announced his candidacy for president. Through a massive nationwide mobilization of supporters and with the support of hard-line conservatives, however, he won the presidency of Iran in 2005.

Ahmadinejad was born on Oct. 28, 1956, in Garmsar, Iran. The son of a blacksmith, he grew up in Tehran and studied to be an engineer at Iran University of Science and Technology, where he was a student leader during the Iranian Revolution. After the revolution, like many of his peers, he joined the Revolutionary Guards, a religious militia group formed by Ayatollah Ruhollah Khomeini. He continued his studies at IUST, eventually earning a doctorate in transportation engineering and planning.

In May 2003, Ahmadinejad was chosen to serve as mayor of Tehran. In that capacity he was credited with solving traffic problems and keeping prices down. As president, he initially focused on issues such as poverty and social justice. He generally took a more conservative approach domestically, in 2005 prohibiting state television and radio stations from broadcasting music considered "indecent," though under his leadership women symbolically were allowed for the first time since the revolution into major sporting events.

Ahmadinejad was very active in foreign affairs, strongly defending Iran's nuclear program against international criticism. Iran's nuclear efforts and Ahmadinejad's provocative foreign policy continued to generate conflict as his term progressed. In September 2007 Ahmadinejad—in New York City to address the United Nations General Assembly—sparked considerable controversy in a speech given at Columbia University in which he suggested the need for further research on the Holocaust and denied the presence of any homosexual individuals in Iran.

Domestically, Ahmadinejad's economic policies also proved to be a trouble spot and became an important campaign issue leading up to the 2009 presidential elections. Election officials indicated that Ahmadinejad won in 2009 with more than 60 percent of the vote. His chief opposition, Mir Hossein Mousavi, and Mousavi's supporters protested the results, claiming electoral irregularities. Demonstrations took place in the capital and elsewhere.

In April 2011 a conflict arose between Ahmadinejad and Ayatollah Ali Khamenei over the dismissal of Iran's minister of intelligence. Ahmadinejad soon found himself facing increased opposition and criticism. The almost unheard-of questioning of a president by the Majles (Iran's legislative body) in 2012 was widely felt to be a sign of Ahmadinejad's lessening political status. This helped further the perception that he would be greatly weakened until the end of his term in 2013.

ALEXANDER THE GREAT

(b. 356 BCE–d. 323 BCE)

More than any other world conqueror, Alexander III of Macedon deserves to be called the Great. Although he died before the age of 33, he conquered almost all the then known world and gave a new direction to history.

Alexander was born in 356 BCE at Pella, the capital of Macedon, a kingdom north of Hellas (Greece). His father was Philip II, under whom Macedon had become strong and united, the first real nation in European history. Alexander was handsome and had the physique of an athlete. He excelled in hunting and loved riding his horse Bucephalus. When Alexander was 13 years old, the Greek philosopher Aristotle came to Macedon to tutor him. He learned something of ethics and politics, as well as the new sciences of botany, zoology, geography, and medicine. His chief interest was military strategy.

Alexander came to the throne in 336 BCE. In the same year he marched southward to Corinth, where the Greek city-states (except Sparta) swore allegiance to him. With Greece secure Alexander prepared to invade Persia.

In the spring of 334 BCE, Alexander crossed the Hellespont (now Dardanelles), the narrow strait between Europe and Asia Minor. He had with him a Greek and Macedonian force of about 30,000 foot soldiers and 5,000 cavalry. Alexander himself led the companions, the elite of the cavalry. With the army went geographers, botanists, and other men of science. A historian kept records of the march, and surveyors made maps that served as the basis for the geography of Asia for centuries.

At the Granicus River in Asia Minor, Alexander defeated a large body of Persian cavalry, four times the size of his own. Then he marched southward along the coast, freeing the Greek cities from Persian rule and making them his allies. Alexander's army and a huge force led by Darius III of Persia met at Issus in October 333 BCE. Alexander charged with his cavalry against Darius, who fled. Late in 332 BCE, Alexander had reached Egypt. The Egyptians welcomed him and accepted him as their pharaoh, or king. Near the delta of the Nile River he founded a new city, to be named Alexandria after him.

In the spring of 331 BCE, Alexander won a great and decisive victory—again against Darius—near the village of Gaugamela, or Camel's House, some miles from the town of Arbela. After the battle he was proclaimed king of Asia. His men wanted to return home, but Alexander was determined to press on to the eastern limit of the world, which he believed was not far beyond the Indus River. He spent the next three years campaigning in the wild country to the east. There he married a chieftain's daughter, Roxane.

In the early summer of 327 BCE Alexander reached India. At the Hydaspes River (now Jhelum) he defeated the army of King Porus. Alexander's men had now marched 11,000 miles (18,000 kilometers). Soon they refused to go farther, and Alexander reluctantly turned back. He had already ordered a fleet built on the Hydaspes, and he sailed down the Indus to its mouth. Then he led his army overland, across the desert. Many died of hunger and thirst.

Alexander reached Susa in the spring of 324 BCE. There he rested with his army. The next spring he went to Babylon. Long marches and many wounds had so lowered his vitality that he was unable to recover from a fever. He died at Babylon on June 13, 323 BCE. His body, encased in gold leaf, was later placed in a magnificent tomb at Alexandria, Egypt.

KOFI ANNAN

(b. 1938–)

T he first black African to hold the post of secretary-general of the United Nations (UN) was Kofi Annan. The career diplomat spoke several African languages, English, and French, and was well respected in the international community

Kofi Atta Annan was born in Kumasi, Ghana, on April 8, 1938. His father was the elected governor of the Ashanti province and was a chief of the Fante people. The younger Annan studied at the University of Science and Technology in Kumasi and won a Ford Foundation grant that enabled him to study in the United States at Macalester College in Minnesota. While studying economics there, in 1960, he won the Minnesota state oratorical contest. He received a postgraduate certificate in economics from the Institute for Advanced International Studies in Geneva, Switzerland.

From 1962 to 1971 Annan worked for the UN as an administration and budget officer with the World Health Organization in Geneva. He received a master's degree in management from the Massachusetts Institute of Technology in 1972, where he was an Alfred P. Sloan fellow. From 1974 to 1976 Annan was managing director of the Ghana Tourist Development Company. Those were his only years away from the UN.

Leading up to his position at the UN's helm, Annan held jobs as assistant secretary-general for program planning, budget, and finance, director of the budget, chief of personnel for the high commissioner for refugees, and administrative officer for the Economic Commission for Africa. When Iraq invaded Kuwait in 1990, Annan was responsible for extricating hundreds of thousands of Asian workers stranded in Kuwait. He was in charge of the UN peacekeeping operations as undersecretary beginning in March 1993. Annan also served as special UN representative to the former Yugoslavia, wherein he was widely praised for his diplomacy in implementing the accord among Bosnian Serbs, Muslims, and Croats. He also led peacekeeping operations in Burundi, Somalia, and Zaire (now the Democratic Republic of the Congo).

After nearly four decades of service to the United Nations, Annan was appointed to lead the organization, marking the first time that a secretary-general was elected from the ranks of the UN staff. He succeeded Boutros Boutros-Ghali in December 1996 as the UN's seventh permanent secretary-general. Annan was elected by acclamation and immediately set to work on a reform plan to be instituted in 1997.

Annan's vision for the UN included peacekeeping and establishing norms for international law, with an emphasis on the values of equality, tolerance, and

Former United Nations secretary-general Kofi Annan. Michael Loccisano/Getty Images

human dignity mandated by the UN charter. He brought a deep commitment for a more efficient and leaner UN and an unyielding advocacy for universal human rights. One of his first challenges as secretary-general was to convince the United States to begin a series of payments to make up the $1.4 billion in debt the country had accumulated. He considered the fight against HIV/AIDS to be a personal priority, and he called for the establishment of a global fund to help increase the flow of money for health care in developing countries.

Annan also used his influence in several political situations; among these were his efforts to convince Iraq to comply with Security Council rulings, as well as his role in effecting the transition to civilian rule in Nigeria. Annan also tried to improve the position of women who worked in the Secretariat of the UN, and he began to build stronger relationships with nongovernmental organizations.

In June 2001, he was unanimously reappointed for a second term as secretary-general. Later that year, the Nobel committee bestowed the Nobel Peace Prize jointly to Annan and the UN on the 100th anniversary of the venerable award. Annan's term ended in 2006. In 2007 he was named chairperson of the Alliance for a Green Revolution in Africa. In 2012, Annan published his autobiography, *Interventions: A Life in War and Peace*, written with Nader Mousavizadeh.

CORAZON AQUINO

(b. 1933–d. 2009)

On Aug. 21, 1983, Benigno Aquino, a Philippine politician opposed to President Ferdinand Marcos, was assassinated as he got off an airplane in Manila. On Feb. 25, 1986, his widow, Corazon Aquino, became the first woman president of the Philippines. In doing so, she ended the 20-year corrupt rule of Marcos.

Born Corazon Cojuangco on Jan. 25, 1933, in Tarlac province, she was raised in a wealthy, politically active family; her father and a brother were both congressmen. She attended school in Manila and in the United States, the latter in Philadelphia and New York City. She graduated from Mount St. Vincent College in New York in 1953.

She met Benigno Aquino after her return to Manila. After their marriage she helped him to pursue his political career. He hoped to be a presidential candidate in the 1973 election, but Marcos imposed martial law in 1972 and imprisoned Benigno Aquino and many other political opponents. After eight years Aquino was released and went into voluntary exile in the United States with Corazon and their five children.

After her husband's death in 1983, Corazon Aquino became more active politically. When Marcos called an election for February 1986, she announced her candidacy. Although results of the election were disputed, Marcos was driven from the country on Feb. 25, 1986, and she assumed the presidency. She immediately released political prisoners and made overtures to Communist revolutionaries.

In the 1992 presidential election Aquino supported retired general Fidel Ramos, her secretary of defense, who had supported her through seven coup attempts. Ramos won the presidency. Aquino died Aug. 1, 2009, at Makati Medical Center in Makati, a suburb of Manila.

YASIR 'ARAFAT

(b. 1929–d. 2004)

The leader of the Palestinian people in their attempt to achieve statehood was Yasir 'Arafat. For his role in helping to negotiate a peace accord between the Palestine Liberation Organization (PLO) and the government of Israel, 'Arafat received the 1994 Nobel Prize for Peace along with Yitzhak Rabin and Shimon Peres of Israel.

'Arafat was born Muhammad 'Abd al-Ra'uf al-Qudwah al-Husayni in August 1929. The day and place of his birth have not been confirmed. 'Arafat attended Cairo University, graduating as a civil engineer. He was president of the Union of Palestinian Students from 1952 to 1956.

'Arafat devoted his life to gaining a permanent homeland for his people, many of whom were displaced in 1948 with the establishment of the State of Israel. He studied guerrilla tactics and joined the Egyptian army, fighting in the Arab-Israeli War of 1956. After the war, 'Arafat moved to Kuwait. There, in 1959, he helped organize Fatah, the largest of the Palestinian guerrilla organizations. This group took control of the PLO in 1969. Under 'Arafat's leadership, the PLO received official recognition from many countries. He addressed the United Nations General Assembly in 1974.

After the 1967 Arab-Israeli War, 'Arafat moved the PLO to Jordan. After the Jordanian army expelled the PLO, it moved its main base to Lebanon, where it continued its attacks against Israel. In 1982 Israel invaded Lebanon and forced the PLO to disperse to various Arab countries.

On November 15, 1988, the PLO under 'Arafat declared an independent Palestinian state in the West Bank and Gaza Strip. In September 1993, after months of secret negotiations in Oslo, Norway, 'Arafat signed a mutual recognition agreement between the PLO and Israel known as the Declaration of Principles. The Oslo accords called for the gradual transfer of power in most of the Israeli-occupied territories of the Gaza

7

Strip and West Bank to the newly created Palestinian Authority (PA) over a five-year period beginning in 1994. The most complex issues were put off until a later date.

In 1996 'Arafat was elected the first president of the PA. Progress toward self-rule stalled in 1997, amid growing distrust between 'Arafat and newly elected Israeli Prime Minister Benjamin Netanyahu, of the right-wing Likud party. In 1998 the two leaders attended a summit in rural Maryland, U.S., where they signed a new peace agreement. Although Netanyahu suspended the agreement in early 1999, 'Arafat signed a further interim agreement with Netanyahu's successor, Ehud Barak, in September. In July 2000 negotiations faltered, and the peace process collapsed. In October 2004 'Arafat became ill and was transferred to Paris, France, for medical treatment. He died in Paris on November 11, 2004.

JEAN-BERTRAND ARISTIDE

(b. 1953–)

The first democratically elected leader of Haiti, Jean-Bertrand Aristide rose from poverty to lead the Haitian people out of more than three decades of political corruption and tyranny. A former parish priest, he advocated for the poor and disenfranchised, earning him the affectionate nickname of Titid, a word that connotes affinity and trust.

Jean-Bertrand Aristide was born on July 15, 1953, in the coastal town of Port-Salut, Haiti. He received his primary education at schools run by the Salesian order and graduated from College Notre Dame in Cap-Haïtien in 1974. Having decided to enter the priesthood, Aristide began his novitiate studies at a Salesian seminary in the Dominican Republic but returned to Haiti to pursue postgraduate studies in philosophy and psychology. In 1979 he traveled to Rome and Israel, spending the next two years studying biblical theology.

Aristide was ordained as a Roman Catholic priest in 1982 and assigned to a parish in one of the poorest sections of Port-au-Prince. He quickly became a leading proponent of *ti legliz*, a progressive movement that advocates spiritual fulfillment through the pursuit of social justice.

8

His passionate sermons, filled with fervent urgings to overturn the elitist and corrupt political structure of the country by using the tactics of nonviolent protest, attracted thousands of congregants. Weekly broadcasts of Aristide's sermons on Radio Soleil carried his message around the country, spreading the seeds of dissent. In 1986 the brutal government of Jean-Claude Duvalier finally fell. However, it was rapidly replaced with a military junta that continued to repress the people. Aristide's outspoken opinions began to endanger his life and those of his congregants. Aristide was formally reprimanded by the diocese and later expelled from the Salesian order.

Despite being stripped of his status as parish priest, Aristide continued to move forward as a champion of the people, listening to their problems and encouraging nonviolent dissent. In 1990 he ran for president and was elected with 67 percent of the vote in what was Haiti's first free election in history. Aristide assumed office in February 1991. His administration was called Lavalas, a Creole word meaning "cleansing," and was aptly named. Aristide's reform of the corrupt civil service, as well as crackdowns on crime and drug trafficking, were largely successful.

Aristide's triumph in attaining political leadership was short-lived, however. On Sept. 30, 1991, the military instituted a violent coup, forcing Aristide into exile. The subsequent campaign of terror perpetrated by the military over the next three years led to thousands of executions, as well as tens of thousands of individuals attempting to flee the country by boat. While in exile, Aristide maintained communication with Haitians around the world and managed to influence the United States, in 1994, to invade Haiti and overturn the violent military regime.

Following the U.S. intervention, Aristide returned to Haiti in October 1994 and resumed his role as president for the final 16 months of his term. He continued to seek improved relations with foreign countries in an attempt to facilitate international aid to the still-impoverished Haitian economy but ran into obstacles when he failed to privatize state-owned industries, a contingency insisted upon by agencies such as the World Bank and the International Monetary Fund. As his term drew to a close, Aristide engaged the United Nations to oversee elections. Barred by the Haiti constitution from seeking a second consecutive term, Aristide promoted his colleague René Préval for the presidency.

Préval was elected and took office in 1996 in the country's first peaceful transition of power from one leader to another.

Aristide ran again for the presidency in 2000 and won, albeit amid considerable controversy concerning voting irregularities surrounding legislative elections held earlier that year. The controversy led the observers and opposition parties to boycott the fall presidential election, leading to questions about the legitimacy of Aristide's election. The resulting instability led to a withdrawal of international support, both financial and political, for Haiti. By mid-2001, however, Aristide pledged to institute electoral reforms. The legislators who had won the controversial seats were asked to resign, and new elections were scheduled.

Although a July 2001 coup against Aristide failed, opposition to his rule increased over the next several years. He fled the country in February 2004 amid anti-government protests that had turned into a full-scale rebellion. He returned in 2011, after seven years of exile.

BASHAR AL-ASSAD

(b. 1965–)

In 2000 Bashar al-Assad became president of Syria, succeeding his father, Hafiz al-Assad. Bashar al-Assad continued his father's authoritarian style of government. Beginning in 2011, he faced a major uprising in Syria that became a civil war.

Bashar was born on September 11, 1965, in Damascus, Syria. His father was a military officer and member of the Ba'ath Party who seized control of Syria in a coup in 1971. Bashar studied medicine at the University of Damascus, graduating in 1988. He served as an army doctor in Damascus, and then moved to England to continue his studies in 1992. When his older brother, who was being groomed to succeed their father as president, was killed in an accident, Bashar was called back to Syria to take his brother's place.

In June 2000 Hafiz al-Assad died, and Bashar was appointed secretary-general of the ruling Ba'ath Party. He was soon elected Syria's president, having run unopposed. Many Syrians objected to the transfer of power from father to son, but it was hoped that his youth, education, and exposure to the West would bring about democratic reform and economic revival. Initially Assad slightly loosened government restrictions on freedom of expression and the press, and released several hundred political prisoners. Those gestures contributed to a brief period of relative openness, dubbed the "Damascus Spring," during which calls for political reform were tolerated. Within months, however, Assad's regime changed course, using threats and arrests to extinguish pro-reform activism. Assad's economic reforms were slight and mainly benefited the politically connected elite.

Assad maintained his father's hard-line stance in Syria's long conflict with Israel. Relations with the United States worsened after Assad denounced the U.S.-led invasion of Iraq in 2003. Syria's relations with Lebanon became strained in 2005, when the Syrian government was widely suspected to be involved in the assassination of a former prime minister of Lebanon, Rafiq al-Hariri. Amid international pressure, Assad withdrew Syrian troops and intelligence services that had long been stationed in Lebanon.

In 2007 Assad was reelected by a nearly unanimous majority to a second term as president of Syria. Critics generally denounced the election. Beginning in March 2011, Assad faced significant challenges when antigovernment protests broke out in Syria, inspired by a wave of pro-democracy uprisings in the Middle East and North Africa. Syrian security forces used lethal force against demonstrators. At first, Assad offered a series of concessions, shuffling his cabinet and then announcing that he would abolish Syria's emergency law and it's Supreme State Security Court, both used to suppress political opposition. As protests spread throughout the country, however, the administration deployed tanks and troops to several Syrian cities. International criticism of Assad's regime mounted amid reports of massacres and indiscriminate violence by security forces.

By September 2011 armed opposition groups had begun to stage increasingly effective attacks against Syrian forces. Attempts at international mediation by the Arab League and the United Nations failed to achieve a cease-fire. By mid-2012 the crisis had evolved into a full-blown civil war that continues still.

KEMAL ATATÜRK

(b. 1881–d. 1938)

As a founder of Turkey and the country's first president, Mustafa Kemal Atatürk presided over the end of the Ottoman Empire. He inaugurated numerous programs of reform to help modernize his country.

Mustafa was born in Salonika, Greece, in 1881. Early in life he decided on a military career. He attended a military secondary school, and for his excellent work in mathematics he took the name Kemal, an Arabic word meaning "perfection." He entered the military academy in Constantinople (now Istanbul) in 1899 and in 1902 the General Staff College. He served in the Italo-Turkish War in 1911–12 and in the Balkan Wars in 1912–13. These wars undermined the 400-year-old Ottoman Empire.

During World War I Kemal opposed Turkey's alliance with Germany. He nevertheless fought for Turkey. His outstanding military abilities and widely circulated political opinions, calling for an independent Turkish state, won him a popular following. He opposed the presence of foreign powers in Turkey and desired an end to the Ottoman Empire.

In 1920, as leader of a

Turkey's founder and leader Kemal Atatürk (foreground, seated). Keystone-France/Gamma-Keystone/Getty Images national resistance movement, he set up a rival government in Ankara. He expelled Greek forces from Asia Minor in 1921–22, and in 1922 he proclaimed the end of the Ottoman Empire. In 1923 he became president of Turkey.

During his presidency Kemal made several changes that affected Turkish life. He proclaimed a secular republic and closed all Islamic religious institutions, including the traditional system of religious education. He abolished the Arabic alphabet and introduced the Latin one. In his effort to align Turkey with the customs of Western nations, he urged the use of Western dress and adopted the use of surnames. He took for himself the name Atatürk, meaning "Father of the Turks." The whole legal system was modernized and a new civil and penal code adopted. Popular forms of entertainment and the use of alcohol were allowed, both normally forbidden in Islamic societies. His attempts to modernize the economy were less successful than his other reforms.

Health problems plagued the last few years of his life. Atatürk died on Nov. 10, 1938, in Istanbul.

ATTILA

(b. 406?–d. 453)

Of all the barbarian leaders who attacked the Roman Empire, none is more famous than Attila the Hun. As king of the Huns, who rose to power in 434 BCE, he exhibited a ferocity that earned him the nickname "scourge of God" in Western Europe.

By the 5th century the Huns ruled a large empire. The Byzantine Empire, which had its capital at Constantinople (now Istanbul, Turkey), had extended its boundaries over too wide an area to stop an invasion at any one point. To keep from being attacked, the Eastern emperor paid an annual tribute to the Huns. The emperor's failure to keep up payments led Attila to invade the Byzantine Empire in two campaigns, in 441–443 and in 447–449. Much of what is now the Balkan region was devastated. The empire lost territory and had to pay a larger tribute.

In 450 Attila claimed Honoria, sister of the Western emperor, Valentinian III, as his wife. As a dowry he expected half of the Western

Empire. To enforce this claim, Attila invaded Gaul (France) in 451. He was defeated and forced to withdraw. In 452 he overran much of northern Italy but turned back before attacking Rome.

His next plan was to lead another invasion of the Byzantine Empire, but he died suddenly after celebrating the last of his marriages. He was succeeded by his sons, who divided his empire.

AUNG SAN

(b. 1915–d. 1947)

B urmese nationalist leader Aung San was instrumental in securing Burma's independence from Great Britain. Before World War II he was actively anti-British, but during the war he switched to the Allies before leading the Burmese drive for autonomy.

Aung San was born Feb. 13, 1915, in Natmauk, Burma (now Myanmar) into a family distinguished in the resistance movement after the British annexation of 1886. He became secretary of the students' union at Rangoon University and, with U Nu, led the students' strike there in February 1936.

After Burma's separation from India in 1937 and his graduation in 1938, he worked for the nationalist Dobama Asiayone ("We-Burmans Association" or "Our Burma Association"), becoming its secretary-general in 1939. While seeking foreign support for Burma's independence in 1940, Aung San received assistance from the Japanese in raising a Burmese military force. Japan actually hoped to use the military troops, known as the "Burma Independence Army," to help them invade Burma for their own gain.

Serving as minister of defense in a Burmese puppet government, Aung San became skeptical of Japanese promises of Burmese independence. Thus, in March 1945, Major General Aung San switched his Burma National Army to the Allied cause.

After the Japanese surrender in August 1945, Aung San and several key members of the victorious Burma National Army formed the People's Volunteer Organization. This was supposed to be a veterans' association interested in social service, but was in fact a private political army designed to be used as a major weapon in the struggle for independence.

In 1946, Aung San used support from the Anti-Fascist People's Freedom League (AFPFL), an underground movement of nationalists he helped form, to become deputy chairman of Burma's Executive Council. In effect he was prime minister, but remained subject to the ruling British governor's veto. On Jan. 27, 1947, after conferring with the British prime minister Clement Attlee in London, he announced an agreement that provided for Burma's independence within one year. In the election for a constitutional assembly in April 1947, his AFPFL won 196 of 202 seats. Though Communists had denounced him as a "tool of British imperialism," he supported a resolution for Burmese independence outside the British Commonwealth.

On July 19, 1947, Aung San and six colleagues, including his brother, were assassinated in the council chamber in Rangoon (now Yangon) while the executive council was in session. His political rival, U Saw, was later executed for his part in the killings.

MENACHEM BEGIN

(b. 1913–d. 1992)

The sixth prime minister of the State of Israel was Menachem Begin. His leadership was characterized by a strong stand in favor of retaining lands captured by Israel in the Arab-Israeli War of 1967. He also opposed the Palestine Liberation Organization (PLO) plan for a Palestinian homeland within or adjacent to Israel.

Menachem Wolfovitch Begin was born on Aug. 16, 1913, in Brest-Litovsk, Russia (now Brest, Belarus). He earned a law degree from the University of Warsaw, Poland, in 1935. Begin received a law degree from the University of Warsaw in 1935. Active in the Zionist (Jewish nationalist) movement throughout the 1930s, he became (1938) the leader of the Polish branch of the Betar youth movement, dedicated to the establishment of a Jewish state on both sides of the Jordan River.

When the Germans invaded Warsaw in 1939, he escaped to Vilnius; his parents and a brother died in concentration camps. The Soviet authorities deported Begin to Siberia in 1940, but in 1941 he was released and joined the Polish army in exile, with which he went to Palestine in 1942.

Begin was commander of the militant Irgun Zvai Leumi in Palestine from 1943 to 1948. He led the opposition in the Israeli Knesset (parliament) from 1948 to 1967 and became joint chairman of the Likud (Unity) coalition in 1970. On May 17, 1977, the Likud Party won a national election, and Begin assumed the post of prime minister on June 21. As prime minister, he was perhaps best known for his uncompromising stand on the question of retaining the West Bank and the Gaza Strip, which had been occupied by Israel during the Arab-Israeli War of 1967.

Prodded by U.S. Pres. Jimmy Carter, however, Begin negotiated with Pres. Anwar el-Sadat of Egypt for peace in the Middle East. The agreements they reached, known as the Camp David Accords (September 17, 1978), led directly to a peace treaty between Israel and Egypt that was signed on March 26, 1979. Under the terms of the treaty, Israel returned the Sinai Penninsula, which it had occupied since the 1967 war, to Egypt in exchange for full diplomatic recognition. Begin and Sādāt were jointly awarded the Nobel Prize for Peace in 1978.

Begin formed another coalition government after the general election of 1981. Despite his willingness to return the Sinai Peninsula to Egypt under the terms of the peace agreement, he remained resolutely opposed to the establishment of a Palestinian state in the West Bank and Gaza Strip. In June 1982 his government mounted an invasion of Lebanon in an effort to oust the Palestine Liberation Organization (PLO) from its bases there. The PLO was driven from Lebanon, but the deaths of numerous Palestinian civilians there turned world opinion against Israel.

In September 1983 Begin suddenly resigned, reportedly because of deteriorating health and depression over his wife's death in 1982. He died on March 9, 1992, in Tel Aviv–Yafo.

DAVID BEN-GURION

(b. 1886–d. 1973)

Statesman and political leader David Ben-Gurion became the first prime minister and chief architect of the State of Israel. He was revered as the "Father of the Nation."

Ben-Gurion was born David Gruen on Oct. 16, 1886, in the town of Plonsk, Poland. His father was a leader in the movement to reclaim Palestine as a home-land for the oppressed Jews of Eastern Europe. The idea of an independent Israel became the leading motiva-tion in Ben-Gurion's life. At age 20 he immigrated to Palestine and worked for several years as a farmer. He adopted the Hebrew name Ben-Gurion and joined the Zionist Socialist movement. At the 1907 Socialist conven-tion he made sure that the party platform contained the statement: "The party aspires to the political independence of the Jewish people in this land."

Israeli leader David Ben-Gurion. Keystone/ Hulton Archive/Getty Images

During World War I Ben-Gurion was expelled from Palestine by the Turks who controlled the region at that time. After the war, when the Turkish Ottoman Empire had ceased to exist, Ben-Gurion returned to Palestine. In 1920 he founded the Histadrut, a confederation of Jewish workers. Ten years later he became president of the Mapai, the Israeli Workers Party.

During World War II Ben-Gurion continued the struggle for an independent Jewish state. In 1948 his efforts were rewarded when the State of Israel was established. His firm policies of defense against Israel's Arab neighbors were worrisome to Britain and the United States, both of which depended on oil from those Arab countries. He was suc-ceeded as prime minister by the more moderate Moshe Sharett in 1953 but returned to office two years later to serve until 1963.

After retiring, Ben-Gurion continued to serve as a member of the Knesset (parliament) until 1970. He died in Tel Aviv on Dec. 1, 1973.

BENAZIR BHUTTO

(b. 1953–d. 2007)

Benazir Bhutto was the first woman to attain political leadership of a Muslim country in modern times. In 1988 she was named prime minister of Pakistan to succeed Gen. Mohammad Zia ul-Haq—the man who had seized the office from her father and ordered his execution.

Bhutto was born on June 21, 1953, in Karachi. She studied abroad, earning degrees from Harvard University, in the United States, in 1973 and the University of Oxford, in England, in 1977. Her father, Zulfikar Ali Bhutto, had led Pakistan since 1971, first as president and then as prime minister, and she often accompanied him on his official travels. In July 1977 his government was overthrown in a revolt led by Zia. Her father was imprisoned and then hanged in 1979. She then became the titular head of her father's political party, the Pakistan People's Party (PPP).

For the next five years Benazir Bhutto was

Former Pakistani Prime Minister Benazir Bhutto, addressing the crowd at a campaign rally. Asif Hassan/AFP/Getty Images

kept either in prison or under house arrest. Zia sent her into exile in London in 1984. After Zia lifted martial law, she returned home to a triumphant welcome in 1986 and became the foremost figure opposing his rule.

After Zia died under mysterious circumstances in a plane crash in August 1988, free elections were held. Bhutto led the PPP to victory and became prime minister of a coalition government in December 1988. She was unable, however, to do much to combat Pakistan's widespread poverty and increasing crime. In August 1990 the country's president, Ghulam Ishaq Khan, dismissed her government on charges of corruption. Her party was defeated in the next elections, and she became the opposition leader in Pakistan's parliament.

In the October 1993 elections, her party won a plurality, and she again became prime minister of a coalition government. Under renewed allegations of corruption and economic mismanagement, however, Bhutto's government was dismissed in 1996 by President Farooq Leghari. Bhutto went into self-imposed exile in 1999 while still facing corruption charges.

Meanwhile, Gen. Pervez Musharraf seized power and became president. In 2007 he finally granted Bhutto amnesty for the corruption charges, and she returned to Pakistan in October of that year. She was assassinated in Rawalpindi on Dec. 27, 2007, as she campaigned for upcoming national elections. Her husband, Asif Ali Zardari, took over as head of the PPP.

Bhutto's autobiography, *Daughter of the East*, was published in 1988. (It was also published under the title *Daughter of Destiny* in 1989.) Her book *Reconciliation: Islam, Democracy, and the West* was published after her death, in 2008.

OTTO VON BISMARCK

(b. 1815–d. 1898)

Under the "iron chancellor," Otto von Bismarck, Germany grew from a weak confederation of states to a powerful empire. For most of the last half of the 19th century, Bismarck's policies controlled the destinies of most of the countries of Europe.

Otto Eduard Leopold von Bismarck-Schönhausen was born on April 1, 1815, at Schönhausen, a family estate in Prussia. He studied law at universities in Göttingen and Berlin, then entered the Prussian civil service. After leaving the service he helped manage the family estates. He entered politics in 1847.

At the time the German states were organized in a loose confederation. Bismarck was determined to free the states from Austrian domination and to unite them under Prussian rule. He first served as a representative at the assembly of the German Confederation and as ambassador to Russia and France. In 1862 he was appointed minister-president of Prussia.

In 1864 Prussia allied with Austria to provoke war with Denmark. The victorious allies won the duchies of Schleswig and Holstein, but two years later quarrels over the duchies led to war between Prussia and Austria. The defeat of Austria gave Prussia control over the states north of the Main River. Bismarck formed them into the North German Confederation.

Relations between Prussia and its age-old enemy France then became tense. In 1870 the nomination of a Hohenzollern prince to the vacant Spanish throne was withdrawn upon French demand. When the French ambassador asked King William I of Prussia to promise that the nomination would never be renewed, the king reacted by dismissing the ambassador. France then declared war on Prussia, and the Prussian army, with the armies of the other German states, attacked and defeated the disorganized French. The German states were then united, and William I became Kaiser, or emperor, of the new German Empire. Bismarck, raised to the rank of prince, became chancellor. During Bismarck's chancellorship, Germany established colonies in Africa and in the Pacific and built up its industries.

William I was succeeded in 1888 by his son Frederick III, a sickly man who ruled only three months. Frederick's son became Kaiser William II. Because William II wanted sole power, he forced Bismarck to resign in 1890. Bismarck retired to his estate at Friedrichsruh, where he died on July 30, 1898.

SIMÓN BOLÍVAR

(b. 1783–d. 1830)

Six nations—Venezuela, Colombia, Panama, Ecuador, Peru, and Bolivia—venerate Simón Bolívar as their liberator from the rule of Spain. Known as the George Washington of South America, he inspired men to follow him through trackless wilderness to fight and die for liberty. Bolívar's followers, however, did not support him as loyally in his struggle to set up stable governments.

Simón Bolívar was born in Caracas (now in Venezuela) on July 24, 1783, of a noble Spanish family. Orphaned in boyhood, he was educated in Europe. He absorbed the spirit of revolution then widespread in Europe and vowed to free Venezuela from Spanish rule.

When Napoleon Bonaparte overran Spain, several colonies of Spanish America seized the opportunity to revolt. Venezuela was the first to declare its independence, in 1811. Although that initial revolt failed, for the next 19 years Bolívar continued to lead the fight to free northern South America. His small, poorly equipped forces won amazing victories and met overwhelming defeats. At the height of his power, between 1825 and 1828, he was president or protector of Gran Colombia (now Venezuela, Colombia, Panama, and Ecuador), Peru, and the newly formed Bolivia.

Bolívar was a sincere patriot, devoted to the cause of liberty and equality. Years before slavery was officially abolished in Venezuela, he had liberated his own slaves. He also was a pioneer in urging the formation of a union of American republics.

The spirit of disunion and opposition remained strong. Bolívar survived an attempt on his life and a revolt staged by one of his own generals. In the fall of 1829, Venezuela seceded from Gran Colombia.

Reluctantly, Bolívar realized that his very existence presented a danger to the internal and external peace of the nations that owed their independence to him. On May 8, 1830, he left Bogotá, planning to take refuge in Europe. Reaching the Atlantic coast, he learned that the person he had trained to be his successor had been assassinated. Bolívar's grief was boundless. The projected trip to Europe was canceled, and, at the invitation of a Spanish admirer, he journeyed to the man's estate near Santa Marta, Columbia. Ironically, his life ended in the house of a Spaniard, where, on Dec. 17, 1830, he died of tuberculosis.

JULIUS CAESAR

(b. 100? BCE–d. 44 BCE)

Assassins ended the career of Julius Caesar before he had finished his lifework. But what he accomplished made him one of the few individuals who changed the course of history.

The date of Caesar's birth has long been disputed, but he was probably born in 100 BCE. He was a patrician by birth, meaning that he belonged to Rome's aristocracy. At the time the Roman republic was the great power in the Mediterranean, but infighting and corruption within the governing elite threatened its supremacy. Caesar's family, despite its noble heritage, sided with the revolutionaries against the nobility. Caesar's political ambitions developed under these circumstances. From the start he probably privately aimed at winning office, not just for personal glory but also to achieve the power to save Rome from decay.

Caesar began to climb the Roman political ladder with his election to the position of Quaestor in 69 or 68. Eventually, in 59, he was elected one of Rome's two consuls, who jointly served as heads of state and held near-absolute authority. To bolster his political standing he formed a political alliance with the wealthy Marcus Licinius Crassus and the popular general Pompey. This alliance became known as the First Triumvirate.

After a year as consul, Caesar was sent to govern a Roman province in Gaul, the region that is now France. From this province he set out to conquer the rest of Gaul, which he accomplished between 58 and 50. This campaign gave Caesar the opportunity to show his great qualities as a leader, an organizer, and a general.

Meanwhile, back in Rome, the triumvirate had begun to collapse. Crassus was killed in battle in Asia Minor in 53, leaving Pompey as sole consul. Pompey, who had grown wary of Caesar's increasing power, sided with Caesar's enemies in the Senate. The Senate ordered Caesar to disband his army but did not demand that Pompey give up his command simultaneously.

Pompey fled across the sea to Greece. Caesar seized the treasury in Rome and set up a temporary government, with himself as dictator. Four years of civil war followed. After a successful campaign in Spain, Caesar sailed for Greece and decisively defeated Pompey at Pharsalus (48 BCE). Pompey fled to Egypt and was murdered there before Caesar could catch up with him. Caesar placed Cleopatra on Egypt's throne and remained with her through the winter. Then he went to Asia Minor and won another victory in Pontus.

In 44 BCE Caesar was powerful enough to have himself made dictator for life. He planned to use his power to put through many far-reaching and much-needed reforms. Sixty senators joined in a conspiracy to assassinate Caesar at a meeting of the Senate on the 15th, or the Ides, of March in 44 BCE. In the group was Caesar's friend Marcus Junius Brutus, a young republican.

Caesar was surrounded by the conspirators in the Senate chamber and attacked. His murder deprived Rome of perhaps its greatest statesman and soldier. Along with his military victories, Caesar's social and political reforms were notable. Shortly before his death Caesar drew up a blueprint for the constitutions of the *municipia*, units of local self-government for Roman citizens.

JIMMY CARTER

(b. 1924–)

In November 1976 Jimmy Carter was elected the 39th president of the United States. His emphasis on morality in government and his concern for social welfare appealed to voters who were disturbed by corruption in government and economic problems.

James Earl Carter, Jr., was born on Oct. 1, 1924, in Plains, a small town in southwestern Georgia. Partly because of the influence of an uncle who was in the navy, Carter decided to attend the United States Naval Academy at Annapolis, Md. In 1943 Carter entered the Naval Academy.

After his graduation he married Rosalynn Smith, the best friend of his sister Ruth. He spent more than six years as a naval officer and qualified as a submarine commander in 1948. By the early 1950s Carter and his wife had three sons, and later, a daughter. Carter had risen to the rank of lieutenant, and a brilliant naval career seemed to be ahead of him.

When Carter's father, a member of the Georgia House of Representatives, died in 1953, Carter decided that he would resign from the navy to pursue a life modeled after his father's.

In 1962 Carter entered the race for the Democratic nomination for the Georgia Senate. He lost by a few votes, partly because of fraud that included stuffed ballot boxes. Carter appealed and was eventually declared the winner. He was reelected in 1964.

In 1966 Carter announced his candidacy for the United States House of Representatives, but he soon shifted his focus to running for governor. He lost the Democratic gubernatorial primary election that year. His next bid for the office was more successful, and in 1971 he was inaugurated as governor of Georgie. He supported integration and appointed many African Americans to posts in state government. He hung portraits of the Rev. Martin Luther King, Jr., and other prominent African Americans in the state Capitol. Carter formed biracial groups to deal with racial tensions.

While serving as chairman of the Democratic Party's 1974 campaign committee, he made wide contacts with other Democratic leaders throughout the country. He began to assemble a campaign staff and advisers. In late 1974 Carter announced that he was a candidate for president.

Carter was strong both in traditionally conservative and in liberal states. He ran well in industrial states as well as farm states. At the Democratic convention in New York City in July 1976 Carter received the nomination on the first ballot. As his vice presidential running mate, he chose Walter F. Mondale, a United States senator from Minnesota.

With the backing of much of the traditional Democratic coalition and with strong support from African Americans and organized labor, Carter won a narrow victory. His 57-vote Electoral College margin was the smallest in 60 years.

Carter tried to establish the image of a president who would stay in touch with the people. He sold the presidential yacht and curtailed

White House limousine service. He conducted a radio phone-in program, *Ask the President*, in which 42 callers—of 9 million who tried to reach him—asked a wide range of questions. Carter established ethics guidelines for Cabinet members and for high-ranking aide.

On Nov. 4, 1979, Iranian militants seized the U.S. Embassy in Tehran and took more than 50 Americans hostage. Carter initiated a series of moves to negotiate the release of the hostages. He called off an unsuccessful military rescue in progress in April 1980. (The last of the hostages were released moments after Carter left office, on Jan. 20, 1981.) He called for a boycott, which more than 60 countries joined, of the 1980 Olympic Games held in Moscow.

Shortly after his election Carter began to lose the support of many liberal Democrats who were critical of his economic policies. He was eventually defeated by the Republican nominee, Ronald Reagan, in one of the worst defeats ever suffered by an incumbent president.

In 1982 he and his wife founded the Carter Center to secure human rights, to resolve conflicts, and to combat disease, hunger, and poverty around the world. He was awarded the Nobel Peace Prize in 2002.

FIDEL CASTRO

(b. 1926–)

The longtime leader of Cuba, Fidel Castro became a symbol of political revolution in the Western Hemisphere. Castro held the title of premier from 1959 until 1976, when he became president of the Council of State and the Council of Ministers.

Fidel Castro Ruz was born on August 13, 1926, on his family's sugar plantation at Mayarí in Oriente Province. As a boy he worked in the sugar fields. He attended Jesuit schools and Belén College in Havana.

Castro entered the University of Havana in 1945. In 1947 he played a minor role in an attempt to overthrow the dictator in the Dominican Republic. He escaped capture and returned to the university to study law, receiving his degree in 1950.

As a Havana lawyer, Castro defended the poor, the oppressed, and people who were in political difficulties. In 1952 he was a candidate

Former Cuban leader Fidel Castro. Sven Creutzmann/Mambo Photo/Getty Images

for the Cuban Congress, but Cuban dictator Gen. Fulgencio Batista canceled the elections. Deciding to act against the Batista regime, Castro and his brother Raúl used their own money to buy guns for about 150 cohorts. On July 26, 1953, they made an unsuccessful assault on the army barracks in Santiago de Cuba. The Castros were sent to prison. Out of this revolt came the name of Castro's organization, the 26th of July Movement.

The Castros were released in 1955. As exiles in New York City and in Mexico, they reorganized their forces. In 1956, with about 80 rebels, they landed in Oriente Province. They were attacked, and most of the rebels were killed. The survivors, including the Castros, escaped into the mountains. For the next two years they waged guerrilla warfare. Batista fled from Cuba in January 1959, and Castro and his army entered Havana.

As premier, Castro declared that Cuba would never again be ruled by a dictator, but it soon became clear that his government was a Communist dictatorship. He had his enemies executed and filled the jails with those suspected of disloyalty to him. The United States severed diplomatic relations with Cuba on Jan. 3, 1961. In April 1961 anti-Castro Cuban exiles backed by the United States government invaded Cuba in an attempt to overthrow the regime. Castro led the forces that defeated them at the Bay of Pigs.

In the fall of 1962 an international crisis arose over the presence of Soviet long-range missiles and bombers in Cuba. Castro was not directly consulted during the negotiations between United States President John F. Kennedy and Soviet Premier Nikita Khrushchev. After Khrushchev agreed to remove the armaments, Castro refused to allow any inspection team to enter Cuba. In December Castro released 1,113 prisoners taken at the Bay of Pigs in return for American food and drugs.

Castro periodically allowed thousands of Cubans to immigrate to the United States after the mid-1960s. His policies remained grounded in Communist theory; though he allowed some economic liberalization and free-market activities while retaining tight control over the country's political life.

On July 31, 2006, while recovering from surgery, Castro passed power on a provisional basis to Raúl. It was the first time since the 1959 revolution that he had ceded control. In February 2008 Castro announced that he was stepping down, officially declaring that he would not accept another term as president of Cuba.

CATHERINE II

(b. 1729–d. 1796)

An obscure German princess became one of the most powerful women in history as Catherine II the Great, empress of Russia. Catherine expanded the territory of Russia and was known for her brilliant court, to which the greatest minds of Europe were drawn.

The future Catherine, christened Princess Sophie Auguste Friederike of Anhalt-Zerbst, was born at Stettin in the Prussian province of Pomerania (now Szczecin, Poland) on May 2, 1729. Early in 1744, when she was almost 15, Sophie was presented to Empress Elizabeth of Russia, who was seeking a wife for her 16-year-old nephew, the Grand Duke Peter, heir to the Russian throne.

Sophie was received into the Russian Orthodox Church and rechristened Catherine (in Russian, Ekaterina). Peter and Catherine were married in 1745. Peter was an immature, sickly youth, and Catherine was bored and unhappy. Her first child, who became Czar Paul I, was born in 1754. In 1757 she had a daughter, Anne, who died in 1758. A son, Alexei, was born in 1762.

When Empress Elizabeth died in January 1762, Peter became Czar Peter III. His childish behavior and his preference for German ways and the Lutheran religion soon made him unpopular. By accepting Russian customs as her own Catherine had gained many supporters, including members of the army. In early July 1762, the army arrested Peter, and Catherine was declared empress. Peter died while in custody.

For years Catherine had studied the works of such French Enlightenment thinkers as Charles de Montesquieu, Denis Diderot, and Voltaire. Her enthusiasm for Western culture led to the flourishing of scholarship, book publishing, journalism, architecture, and the theater. Catherine herself wrote articles and plays. She sponsored the first school for girls in Russia and established a system of elementary schools. After the French Revolution, however, she became critical of liberal attitudes.

Although Catherine was eager to be considered progressive, many of her social policies were reactionary. Between 1767 and 1768 she sponsored a commission to codify Russian laws, only to cancel the project when the delegates produced no results.

After a peasant rebellion in 1773–74, she instituted a new system of local government that strengthened the power of the local landlords. Under her Charter to the Nobility of 1785, the landlord's control over peasants and serfs became stronger than ever before.

Catherine fought two wars with Turkey, from 1768 to 1774 and from 1787 to 1792. As a result, Russia won part of the northern Black Sea coast, the Crimean peninsula, and navigation rights in Turkish waters. She also joined with Prussia and Austria in partitioning Poland in 1772, 1793, and 1795. She was extremely ambitious and hoped to conquer even more territory, but these plans were not realized by the time she died on Nov. 17, 1796.

CHARLEMAGNE

(b. 742?–d. 814)

The man now known as Charlemagne became king of the Franks in 768. Within a few decades his conquests had united almost all the

Christian lands of Western Europe into one state, which became known as the Holy Roman Empire. His name means "Charles the Great." His vast empire did not remain intact for long after his death, but during his reign the traditions of civilization were revived after having been almost forgotten.

Charlemagne belonged to the Carolingians, a particularly powerful branch of the Franks. The Franks, for whom France is named, took advantage of the collapse of the original Roman Empire to extend their domain from what is now Germany into other parts of Western Europe.

Charlemagne's grandfather was Charles Martel, a noted warrior who claimed the entire Frankish kingdom for himself. Charlemagne's father was Pippin the Short and his mother was Bertrade. Although schools had almost disappeared in the 8th century, historians believe that Bertrade gave young Charles some education and that he learned to read. He also became devoted to the church, and that devotion motivated him throughout his life.

In 771 Charlemagne became sole ruler of the kingdom of the Franks. He was determined to strengthen his realm and to bring order to Europe. In 772 he launched a 30-year campaign that conquered and brought Christianity to the powerful Saxons in the north.

The key to Charlemagne's conquests was his ability to organize. During his reign he sent out more than 50 military expeditions and rode as commander at the head of at least half of them. He moved his armies very quickly over wide reaches of country, but every move was planned in advance. His feats of organization and the swift marches later led the emperor Napoleon to study his tactics.

By 800 Charlemagne was the undisputed ruler of Western Europe. His vast realm covered what are now France, Switzerland, Belgium, and the Netherlands. It included half of present-day Italy and Germany, part of Austria, and the Spanish March ("border"). By thus establishing a central government over Western Europe, Charlemagne restored much of the unity of the old Roman Empire and paved the way for the development of modern Europe.

On Christmas Day in 800 Charlemagne went to mass at St. Peter's Basilica in Rome and was acclaimed by the throng of worshippers. On this occasion Pope Leo III placed a golden crown upon his head and proclaimed him to be emperor of the West. The coronation was the foundation of the Holy Roman Empire. Though Charlemagne did not use the title, he is considered the first Holy Roman emperor.

Charlemagne had deep sympathy for the peasants and believed that government should be for the benefit of the governed. He set up money standards to encourage commerce and urged better farming methods. He especially worked to spread education and Christianity in every class of people. An impressive monument to his religious devotion is the cathedral at Aachen, which he built and where he was buried. He died in 814.

HUGO CHÁVEZ

(b. 1954–d. 2013)

Former Venezuelan President Hugo Chávez styled himself as the leader of the "Bolivarian Revolution," a socialist political program for much of Latin America. The revolution was named for the South American independence hero Simón Bolívar. Chavez had a form of political reform named for himself as well; his ideology became known to many as simply *chavismo*.

Hugo Rafael Chávez Frías was born on July 28, 1954, in Sabaneta, Barinas, Venezuela. His parents, both schoolteachers, did not have enough money to support all their children, so Hugo and his eldest brother, Adán, were raised in the city of Barinas by their grandmother, Rosa Inés Chávez, who instilled in Hugo a love of history and politics.

As a teenager, Chávez was heavily influenced by the teachings of Bolívar and Karl Marx, the German philosopher who was one of the fathers of Communism. Both Bolívar and Marx had a profound impact on Chávez's political philosophy, as did Cuban leader Fidel Castro, who would later become Chávez's political muse.

In 1971 Chavez entered the Venezuelan Military Academy in the capital city of Caracas, not because he wanted to be a soldier but because he dreamed of becoming a professional baseball player; the academy had good baseball coaches. He was a poor and unruly student, and ultimately graduated near the bottom of his class in 1975.

His first assignment as a second lieutenant in the army was to capture the remaining leftist guerrillas. But as he pursued the insurgents, Chávez began to empathize with them, seeing them as peasants fighting for a better life. In 1982 Chávez and some fellow military officers secretly formed the Bolivarian Movement 200, which spread the peasants' revolutionary ideology within the military.

On February 4, 1992, Chávez and a group of military officers led an attempt to overthrow the government of Pres. Carlos Andrés Pérez. The rebellion quickly collapsed. Trapped in the Military History Museum near the presidential palace, Chavez agreed to surrender on the condition that he be allowed to address his co-conspirators on national television. Chávez told his fellow "comrades" that regrettably—"for now," he said—their goal of taking power could not be accomplished, and he beseeched them to put down their arms to avoid further bloodshed. His address became known as the *por ahora* ("for now") speech because many people took that specific phrase as a promise that one day Chávez would return.

Chávez was imprisoned without a court ruling for the attempted coup until 1994, when Pres. Rafael Caldera Rodríguez, bowing to Chávez's growing popularity, dropped the charges against him. Chávez then founded the political party Movement of the Fifth Republic (Movimiento de la Quinta República; abbreviated MVR), enlisting many former socialist activists and military officers. In December 1998, running as the MVR candidate, he won the presidential election with 56 percent of the vote.

Chávez's early platform—which supported an end to corruption, increased spending on social programs, and redistribution of the country's oil wealth—was widely applauded. Chávez then oversaw the drafting of a new constitution that gave him unprecedented control over the three branches of government. He continued to pass controversial laws by decree and moved to limit the independent press. By early 2002 anti-Chávez marches had become regular occurrences.

On April 11, 2002, one such rally turned violent. A battle broke out between marchers and pro-Chávez gunmen and National Guard troops, which sparked a military revolt. In a move widely condemned as illegal, the military took Chávez into custody. The following day the military established a temporary government. However, they withdrew their support when the interim president dissolved most of Venezuela's democratic institutions and suspended the constitution. On April 13 Chávez's vice president, Diosdado Cabello, was recognized as the rightful successor. Once sworn in, Cabello restored Chávez to power, and Chávez returned to the presidential palace on the morning of April 14.

The restoration was the first of a string of conflicts between the Chávez government and the opposition. In December 2002 the opposition began a national strike designed to force Chávez to resign. Despite allegations of fraud, Chávez defeated a recall vote in August 2004. In December 2005, to protest what they felt was a corrupt election process, opposition candidates boycotted the country's legislative elections. Despite the ongoing conflict, Chávez was elected president for a third time in 2006, with 63 percent of the vote.

In June 2011 Chávez was operated on in Cuba to remove a cancerous tumor. Although speculation grew as to whether he would be physically able to stand for reelection in 2012, he mounted an aggressive campaign against challenger Henrique Capriles Radonski and won in October. In December 2012 Chávez underwent his fourth cancer surgery in Cuba. He was not well enough to return to Venezuela for his scheduled January 2013 inauguration. Eventually, Chávez made his way back to Caracas, where he died on March 5, 2013.

CHIANG KAI-SHEK

(b. 1887–d. 1975)

The lifelong dream of Gen. Chiang Kai-shek was for China to be united and free of foreign domination. As the military and civilian leader of the Republic of China, first on the Asian mainland and later on the island of Taiwan, General Chiang became one of the most controversial men of his time.

Chiang was born on Oct. 31, 1887, in Zhejiang Province. He trained for a military career from a young age, first in northern China and then at the Military Staff College in Japan. In Japan Chiang was attracted to the teachings of the exiled Chinese revolutionary leader Sun Yat-sen. Sun

and his followers wanted to overthrow the Manchus, a group that
had controlled China since the 17th
century, and to establish a republic.
In 1911 Chiang returned to China
and took part in the revolt that
accomplished that goal.

In 1913, with the new republic
governed by a would-be dictator,
Chiang joined in an unsuccessful revolt. This cost him his army
post. After the death of the dictator in 1916 various leaders and
warlords struggled for power in the
country. Sun Yat-sen, leader of the
Kuomintang (Nationalist Party),
tried to unify the country. In 1923
he sent Chiang to Moscow to study
Soviet military and political institutions. On his return Chiang became

Chinese leader Chiang Kai-shek.
Topical Press Agency/Hulton Archive/
Getty Images

the director of a military academy at Canton (Guangzhou).

After Sun's death in 1925, Chiang rose to power in the Kuomintang
and took command of the revolutionary army in 1926. The general then
began advancing to the north of China, with Beijing, capital of the weak
republic, as his goal. In a 1,200-mile (1,900-kilometer) march, he gained
control of south and central China. During this period Chiang took two
steps that were to have major consequences for the country and his own
life. Alarmed by the growth of Communism, he dismissed his Soviet
advisers and expelled the Communists from his party. He also married
the American-educated Soong Mei-ling. Known as Madame Chiang,
she became her husband's close adviser.

In 1928 Chiang's army entered Beijing and, as chief of the Kuomintang,
he became the head of the Republic of China. Nanjing (Nanking), to the
south, was made the new capital.

China, however, was still far from unified. For years Chiang battled
insurgent regional commanders and armed Communist forces. When

Japan invaded Manchuria in 1931, Chiang offered no resistance, as he believed China still too weak to risk a war. Widespread criticism forced him to resign as head of the nation, but he continued as commander of the army.

Chiang speeded his program for unifying and strengthening China. In 1935 he launched the New Life movement—a program designed to improve the lot of the peasants through education, home industries, and self-help. Its goal was to halt the spread of Communism by teaching traditional Chinese values.

When Japan again invaded China in an undeclared war, Chiang was forced to form a temporary alliance with the Communists. His forces kept most of China free of Japanese control and managed to move industries and schools to the interior. After the Allied forces declared war against Japan during World War II, Chiang became Allied commander in China. He became China's president in 1943. China received economic aid from the United States, but Chiang did not push economic or political reforms. Much of his Nationalist government was corrupt, and inflation brought increasing hardship to the masses.

Chiang did not actively resist the Japanese during World War II. It is thought that this strategy cost him the support of many Chinese people and demoralized his own troops. As a result, when fighting between the Communists and Chiang's forces resumed at the end of the war, the Chinese Communists advanced steadily. By 1949 they had won the entire mainland and established the People's Republic of China.

Chiang escaped to the island of Taiwan and set up a government there called the Republic of China. With the support of the United States, he controlled China's seats in the United Nations General Assembly and Security Council until 1971. Chiang remained president of the Republic of China until his death on April 5, 1975.

WINSTON CHURCHILL

(b. 1874–d. 1965)

Once called "a genius without judgment," Sir Winston Churchill rose through a stormy career to become an internationally respected statesman during World War II. He was one of Britain's greatest prime ministers.

Winston Leonard Spenser Churchill was born on Nov. 30, 1874, at Blenheim Palace, the estate of the dukes of Marlborough. When Winston was born, his father was chancellor of the exchequer for Queen Victoria. When he was 16, he entered Sandhurst, a historic British military college.

In March 1895 he became a sub-lieutenant in the 4th (Queen's Own) Hussars, a distinguished cavalry regiment. He joined a Punjab Infantry regiment in India in 1897. Between duties he read the

British Prime Minister Winston Churchill, leaving his residence at 10 Downing St. in London during World War II. Popperfoto/Getty Images

works of Gibbon, Darwin, Plato, Aristotle, Schopenhauer, and Macaulay. From Gibbon especially, Churchill learned much of the sonorous, rich style that was to make him the outstanding orator of his day. In 1898 he joined the British army in the Sudan.

Churchill's return to England in 1899 changed his career. Disliking his low army salary, he determined to enter politics. But when he "stood" for Parliament, he was defeated. Churchill was undaunted.

At the outbreak of the Boer War in South Africa in 1899, he obtained an assignment from the *Morning Post* as war correspondent. Churchill rode into the thick of firing at Spion Kop, Vaal Krantz, and other ensuing battles. In one engagement he was captured by Louis Botha and imprisoned with others in Pretoria.

Upon his return to England, Churchill made up for an old defeat, as he was to do so often in his life. The same men who had rejected him earlier now elected him to Parliament as a hero in 1900.

In his first term in Parliament, Churchill soon showed that he was to be a highly individual politician. Though elected as a Conservative, he showed little awe of any party leader. He soon changed from Conservative to Liberal and in 1906 was returned to Parliament as a Liberal member from Manchester.

Even Churchill's foes could not deny that he was a hard worker with enormous energy. At 32 he became undersecretary of state for the colonies (1906–8). Two years later he entered the Cabinet as president of the board of trade (1908–10). He also served as secretary of state for home affairs (1910–11).

England feared war with Germany after the Agadir incident in July 1911. Churchill was made first lord of the admiralty and ordered to put the fleet into a state of instant readiness. From that moment, Churchill worked hard to reorganize the navy. He built a fine staff, obtained 15-inch guns and fast battleships, and developed the Royal Naval Air Service, which was the forerunner of the Royal Air Force. When World War I broke out three years later, Churchill's efficient navy became England's first powerful weapon against Germany.

In 1915, however, Churchill again met failure. As a war adviser, he led a small group in advocating an attack on the Gallipoli peninsula. The campaign, which was designed to eliminate Turkey from the war, proved a disastrous failure.

Churchill resigned his post under sharp criticism. He then went to France as a lieutenant colonel. His ability to get things done, however, was badly needed and in 1917 he was made minister of munitions in wartime England.

The years between the first and second World Wars found Churchill gradually slipping from power. England, exhausted by war, only called him a warmonger when he raised his voice in Parliament after the Lausanne Disarmament Conference in 1932. However, from the moment that Hitler rose to power in Germany in 1933, Churchill, again a Conservative, saw the challenge. He gathered data on German rearmament, trying to waken England. In 1938, when Prime Minister Neville Chamberlain sacrificed Czechoslovakia to appease Hitler, Churchill warned him of an impending war.

On Sept. 3, 1939, war came. Chamberlain at once appointed Churchill to his former post as first lord of the admiralty. Eight months later, on May 10, 1940, Chamberlain was forced to resign as prime minister. Churchill succeeded him.

At the moment Churchill took office, the armed might of Germany was sweeping Europe. Yet Churchill stood firm before the British people. His thundering defiance and courage heartened Britain, and his two fingers raised in the "V for Victory" sign became an international symbol for determination and hope.

Before the United States entered the war, he obtained American destroyers and lend-lease aid and met with President Franklin D. Roosevelt in 1941 to draw up the Atlantic Charter. Later he helped plan overall Allied strategy. The Labor Party won the general election of 1945, forcing Churchill's resignation as prime minister.

Churchill's flair for colorful speech endured. His phrase "Iron curtain" soon became the term for the barrier between the West and areas under Soviet control. In 1951 Churchill was again chosen prime minister, resigning in 1955. In 1953 he was knighted by Queen Elizabeth II and received the Nobel Prize for Literature.

Since 1908 Churchill had been married to the former Clementine Ogilvy Hozier. They had one son and three daughters. Churchill died in London on Jan. 24, 1965. He received a state funeral, the first for a commoner since 1898. He was buried at Bladon, near Blenheim Palace.

CLEOPATRA

(b. 69 BCE–d. 30 BCE)

One of the most fascinating women of all time was Cleopatra VII, queen of Egypt. She had great intelligence and beauty, and she used both to further Egypt's political aims.

Cleopatra was of Greek heritage and culture, one of the Ptolemy line set on the throne of Egypt after the conquest of Alexander the Great. Her father, Ptolemy XII, named her and his elder son, Ptolemy, joint rulers. Cleopatra came to the throne in 51 BCE. Three years later young Ptolemy's supporters had Cleopatra driven into exile.

In 48 BCE Caesar appeared in Egypt in pursuit of his rival, Pompey. When Cleopatra heard that Caesar was in the palace in Alexandria, she had one of her attendants carry her to him, rolled up in a rug offered as a gift. Captivated by her charm, the 52-year-old Roman helped her regain her throne. Ptolemy XIII was drowned, and Caesar made Cleopatra's younger brother, Ptolemy XIV, joint ruler with her.

Cleopatra bore Caesar a son, called Caesarion, meaning "little Caesar." When Caesar returned to Rome, she followed him with their baby and lived in Caesar's villa, where he visited her constantly. After Caesar was assassinated in 44 BCE, Cleopatra returned to Egypt. Soon after, Ptolemy XIV died, perhaps poisoned by Cleopatra, and the queen named her son Caesarion co-ruler with her as Ptolemy Caesar.

Civil war followed Caesar's assassination, and the Roman Empire was divided. Mark Antony, as ruler of the eastern empire, summoned Cleopatra to Tarsus, in Asia Minor, to answer charges that she had aided his enemies. The queen arrived, dressed as Venus, on a magnificent river barge. She welcomed Antony with feasting and entertainment. Fascinated by her, he followed her to Alexandria.

After a festive winter with Cleopatra, Antony returned to Rome. He married Octavia, sister of Octavian (later called Augustus), though he still loved Cleopatra, who had borne him twins. When he went east again, in an expedition against the Parthians, he sent for her and they were married.

Octavian was furious and declared war on Cleopatra. Antony and Cleopatra assembled 500 ships. Octavian blockaded them off the west coast of Greece, and the famous 31 BCE Battle of Actium followed. Cleopatra slipped through the blockade and Antony followed her, but his fleet surrendered.

The next year Octavian reached Alexandria and again defeated Antony. Cleopatra took refuge in the mausoleum she had had built for herself. Antony, informed that Cleopatra was dead, stabbed himself. Soon another messenger arrived, saying Cleopatra still lived. Antony insisted on being carried to her and died in her arms. Later Cleopatra committed suicide—tradition says by the bite of a poisonous asp, which is a type of snake.

CONSTANTINE I

(b. 280?–d. 337)

Constantine I was the first Roman emperor to profess Christianity. He not only initiated the evolution of the empire into a Christian state but also provided the impulse for a distinctively Christian culture that prepared the way for the growth of Byzantine and Western medieval culture.

Constantine was born on February 27, probably in the later 280s CE, in Naissus, Moesia (now Niš, Serbia). He was brought up in the Eastern Empire at the court of the senior emperor Diocletian at Nicomedia (modern İzmit, Turkey). Constantine was acclaimed emperor by the army in 306. He then threw himself into a complex series of civil wars, after which he became Western emperor.

Constantine met with Eastern emperor Licinius at Mediolanum (modern Milan) to confirm a number of political and dynastic arrangements. A product of this meeting has become known as the Edict of Milan, which extended toleration to the Christians and restored any personal and corporate property that had been confiscated during the persecution. But Constantine went far beyond the joint policy agreed upon at Mediolanum. By 313 he had already donated to the bishop of Rome the imperial property of the Lateran. In 324, Constantine battled Licinius and won, becoming sole emperor of East and West.

Constantine's visited the West in 326, to celebrate the anniversary of his reign. His refusal to take part in a pagan procession offended the Romans. When he left after a short visit, it was never to return. During his absence from the East, a scandal broke out back home. For reasons that remain obscure, Constantine had his eldest son, the deputy emperor Crispus, and his own wife Fausta, Crispus's stepmother, slain. These events set the course of the last phase of the reign of Constantine.

Immediately upon his return from the West he began to rebuild the city of Constantinople (fomerly Byzantium) on a greatly enlarged pattern, as his permanent capital and the "second Rome." The dedication of Constantinople (May 330) confirmed a split between the emperors and Rome, which had been in the making for more than a century.

Constantine's interest in church building was expressed also in Constantinople. In Rome, the great church of St. Peter was begun in the later 320s and lavishly endowed by Constantine with plate and property. The emperor was an earnest student of his religion. In later years he commissioned new copies of the Bible for the growing congregations at Constantinople. He issued numerous laws favorable to Christians and the practice of their religion; he abolished the penalty of crucifixion and the practice of branding certain criminals, and ordered the observance of Sunday and saints' days.

Constantine had hoped to be baptized in the Jordan River, but the ceremony was delayed until the end of his life. He fell ill at Helenopolis and was forced to take to his bed near Nicomedia when treatment failed. There, Constantine received baptism. He died on May 22, 337, in Ancyrona, near Nicomedia, Bithynia (now İzmit, Turkey). He was buried at Constantinople in his church of the Apostles, whose memorials, six on each side, flanked his tomb.

OLIVER CROMWELL

(b. 1599–d. 1658)

The chief leader of the Puritan Revolution in England was Oliver Cromwell, a soldier and statesman. He joined with the Puritans to preserve Protestantism and the law against the tyranny of King Charles I. Cromwell was made lord protector of the Commonwealth of England, Scotland, and Ireland in December 1653 and held that office until his death five years later.

Cromwell was born on April 25, 1599, at Huntingdon, in eastern England. His father was a well-to-do farmer. When Oliver was 17 he entered nearby Cambridge University, but returned home the following year to farm the lands he had inherited on his father's death. He married Elizabeth Bourchier, the daughter of a wealthy London merchant, in 1620.

When he was 29, Cromwell was elected to Parliament. King Charles dismissed this Parliament the next year and for 11 years ruled as a despot without calling Parliament at all. Finally in 1640 he was forced to call it again. Cromwell was once more a member of this Parliament. He immediately became important to the Puritan cause because of his strong religious beliefs and the vigor with which he defended civil and religious liberties against the king.

The people, particularly the Puritans, were gradually aroused to seek the overthrow of the king's unchecked rule. Early in 1642, when civil war was in sight, Cromwell returned to his home and set about raising, equipping, and training a "troop of horse" (meaning cavalry soldiers). His men were full of religious fervor, each soldier carrying a Bible as an important part of his equipment.

Cromwell would not allow Roman Catholics in his army, but he accepted devout God-fearing believers from all the Protestant churches. For the time in which he lived, this was considered religious tolerance. His commitment to the Puritan cause colored his whole career as soldier and statesman. The quality of Cromwell's troop of horse was first proved at Marston Moor, near York, in July 1644. He was named "Ironsides" for his ability.

As the civil war dragged on, Cromwell became more and more prominent. He even led a movement for remaking the parliamentary army as a whole on the model of his own Ironsides. He again won an important and decisive victory over the king's forces at the Battle of Naseby in June 1645. King Charles, left almost defenseless, gave himself up early in the following year to the Scots, who had been cooperating with the English to overthrow despotism. Because Charles was a Scot, he thought he could come to some agreement with them. The Scots, however, turned Charles over to the English.

England was now ruled by the army and its great leader and by that part of the Parliament of 1640 that was loyal to the Puritan ideals. This remnant, the "sitting" members of Parliament, was jokingly called the "Rump." Both the Rump and the army came to feel that Charles was so untrustworthy and autocratic that he must be eliminated. The king was tried and beheaded in 1649.

The Rump thereupon proclaimed the whole of the British Isles a republic under the name of the Commonwealth. The Scots, however, now wanted Stuart rule, and crowned Charles II, the young son of Charles I. The Irish, who were largely Roman Catholic, also resisted Parliament's authority.

Cromwell, now commander in chief of the army, brought the Scots to submission at the Battle of Dunbar in 1650 and again the next year at Worcester. He had crushed the Irish in a campaign that climaxed in the storming of Drogheda in 1649.

Cromwell dismissed the Rump in 1653 when it fell out with the army. Not long after, he became the head of the Commonwealth under the title of lord protector. For the next five years he ruled the British Isles. Toleration was granted to all Protestants. The Jews, who had been legally banned from the country for more than 300 years, were allowed in England again and permitted to carry on their worship privately. The navy was made more powerful, and the government gained great respect abroad.

Cromwell's rule was not a long one. He died peacefully in his bed on Sept. 3, 1658. Much that Cromwell fought for was swept away in 1660 when the Stuart rule was resumed by Charles II; yet the protector's work was not altogether in vain. As the British developed more liberal views in both church and state, the example of Cromwell and his pro-tectorate was not forgotten by them.

DALAI LAMA XIV

(b. 1935–)

To Tibetan Buddhists, a Dalai Lama is the living form of the lord of compassion who takes earthly forms in order to help human-kind. The title is often translated as "Ocean of Wisdom." Since the mid-17th century, the Dalai Lama has been the spiritual leader of Tibet-an Buddhism. Until the mid-20th century, when the 14th Dalai Lama,

Tenzin Gyatso, was forced into exile, the Dalai Lama also ruled Tibet politically.

Tenzin Gyatso was born as Lhamo Thondup on July 6, 1935, in the village of Taktser, Qinghai province, China. His parents were peasants of Tibetan birth.

Each Dalai Lama is seen as a rebirth of the first of the line. After the death of a Dalai Lama, monks begin what may be a long search for the child believed to be the new incarnation, guided by various other signs. Tenzin Gyatso was identified as the 14th Dalai Lama in 1937 and enthroned in 1940. He received an extensive education, and in 1959 he earned a degree equivalent to a doctorate in Buddhist philosophy.

The Dalai Lama, preparing to speak to Japanese lawmakers in Tokyo, 2012. Toru Yamanaka/AFP/Getty Images

The Dalai Lama assumed his full role as ruler of Tibet on November 17, 1950, at age 15. A month later he fled the advance of Chinese troops, which had entered Tibet in 1949. He returned to Lhasa in 1951 and spent several unsuccessful years attempting to make a peaceful and workable arrangement with China.

In 1959 the Chinese crushed an attempted revolution, killing tens of thousands of Tibetans. The Dalai Lama fled along with about 100 followers. They eventually settled in the Himalayas, in Dharmsala, India. There the Dalai Lama created a government-in-exile and waged a peaceful campaign to end the Chinese military presence. For his efforts, he was awarded the Nobel Peace Prize in 1989.

The Dalai Lama traveled widely, teaching, lecturing, and meeting with many world leaders. Wherever he went, he spoke out against Chinese abuses of Tibetans and the destruction of Tibetan culture. The first Dalai Lama to become a global public figure, he became a spokesman not only for his people but for Tibetan Buddhism.

DENG XIAOPING

(b. 1904–d. 1997)

During the Cultural Revolution of the 1960s, China's Communist government publicly humiliated former vice-premier Deng Xiaoping by parading him through the national capital in a dunce cap. Yet, after the death of Mao Zedong in 1976, he emerged as his country's paramount leader. Deng was acclaimed as a reformer who resisted rigid Communist ideology, introduced elements of free enterprise, and helped restore stability and economic growth. His international image was tarnished in mid-1989, however, when he ordered a military crackdown on pro-democracy protesters.

He was born Deng Xixian on Aug. 22, 1904, to a wealthy family in Sichuan Province. At age 16 he went to Paris to study. While there he joined the Communist movement and was befriended by Zhou Enlai. He went to the Soviet Union to study in 1926. The following year Deng returned to China and began to work actively as an underground organizer for the Communist Party, becoming a close adviser to Mao during the Chinese civil war.

Deng became a vice-premier in 1952. By the mid-1950s he was a member of the ruling Political Bureau and general secretary of the Chinese Communist Party. His plans for the country's economic growth stressed that pay given to industrial workers and farmers should be linked more clearly to their efforts. This and other positions brought him into conflict with Chairman Mao, and during the Cultural Revolution he was condemned by radical Maoists.

Deng was rehabilitated under Premier Zhou in 1973. As the most senior vice-premier, Deng became the effective head of the government during Zhou's later illness. Instead of succeeding Zhou when the premier died in 1976, Deng was banished by the radical Gang of Four, an elite group of Mao's supporters.

After Mao's death, the Gang of Four lost power, and Deng was again reinstated to his powerful positions. For a few years Deng struggled for supreme control with Hua Guofeng, Mao's chosen successor. But in 1980–81 Deng engineered the promotions of his own protégés—Zhao Ziyang as premier and Hu Yaobang as party chairman—to replace Hua.

Deng then became the country's chief policy maker, instituting a wide array of economic and social reforms, including a strict family-planning program to combat population growth. He also strengthened the country's ties to Western nations and encouraged foreign investment in China. In late 1987, to force the resignation of senior leaders who opposed his policies, Deng gave up his own committee posts. He retained his very powerful position as chairman of the party's Central Military Commission until 1989.

In early 1987 Zhao had ousted Hu, whose support of Western-style democracy had been blamed for a rash of student demonstrations for political freedom. Hu's death in April 1989 became the catalyst for more-aggressive pro-democracy demonstrations. In June, Deng approved the use of force to put down demonstrations in Beijing's Tiananmen Square, which ended in the army's massacre of hundreds of unarmed marchers. The aging Deng resigned from his last official party post in 1989 but remained influential until his death on February 19, 1997 in Beijing.

EAMON DE VALERA

(b. 1882–d. 1975)

U.S.-born Irish politician and patriot Eamon de Valera became one of Ireland's greatest leaders in its struggle for independence. After the country was freed from British rule in 1922, he led it from 1932 to 1948, first as president of the executive council and later as prime minister. After the Republic of Ireland was proclaimed, he served two terms as its prime minister before he was elected president in 1959 and in 1966.

Edward de Valera was born in New York City on October 14, 1882. His father was Spanish, and his mother was Irish. When the boy was

45

two years old his father died, and Edward went to live with his grand-mother in County Limerick, Ireland. In school he was a good student and athlete, especially in track. At the age of 16 he won a scholar-ship to Blackrock College in Dublin. In 1904 he earned a degree in mathematics at Royal University, now the National University of Ireland.

For years de Valera gave little thought to politics. He taught at sev-eral schools. He also joined the Gaelic League, which aimed to revive Irish culture and the ancient Gaelic language. In 1910 he married Jane O'Flanagan, a teacher of Gaelic. They later adopted the Gaelic versions of their names—Eamon and Sinead.

In 1913 de Valera joined the Irish Volunteers, an underground army pledged to fight British rule. During the anti-British Easter Rising in April 1916, de Valera led a group of 100 and was the last commander to surrender. All the leaders of the uprising were executed except de Valera. His life was spared because of his American birth, but he was sentenced to jail. In 1917 the British released all political prisoners. Later that year, as the chief survivor of the Easter Rising, de Valera was elected presi-dent of the Irish revolutionary Sinn Fein ("We Ourselves" or "Ourselves Alone") Party.

Again jailed for revolutionary activity, de Valera escaped to the United States in 1919 and raised millions of dollars for the Irish cause. Returning to Ireland before the end of the Anglo-Irish War (Irish War of Independence), he opposed the conditions set by the Anglo-Irish Treaty of 1921 that formed the Irish Free State, mainly because it required an oath of allegiance to the British crown. De Valera's repub-lican group fought the Free State government, and in 1923 he was again sent to prison but was released by the next year. The Sinn Fein returned him to Parliament in 1924, but the party split on taking the oath of allegiance to the king. In 1926 de Valera formed a new party, Fianna Fail ("Soldiers of Destiny"). It won control of Parliament in 1932, and de Valera became president of the executive council. In that capacity, he worked to sever connections with Great Britain. In 1937, largely through de Valera's efforts, the Irish Free State became Ireland, a sover-eign, independent democracy linked with the British Commonwealth only for purposes of diplomatic representation.

De Valera's prestige was enhanced by his success as president of the council of the League of Nations in 1932 and of its assembly in 1938. In 1937 he became prime minister of Ireland, an office he again held from 1951 to 1954 and from 1957 to 1959. He was elected president in 1959 and reelected in 1966. De Valera retired to a nursing home near Dublin in 1973 and died there on August 29, 1975.

FRANÇOIS DUVALIER AND JEAN-CLAUDE DUVALIER

François Duvalier (b. 1907–d. 1971)
Jean-Claude Duvalier (b. 1951–)

The president of Haiti from 1957 to 1971, François Duvalier was often referred to as "Papa Doc" because he had begun his career as a physician. During his 14 years in power in one of the poorest countries in the world, he used violence and terror to stop all who opposed him. Before his death in 1971, he designated his 20-year-old son, Jean-Claude Duvalier, called "Baby Doc," to succeed him as president.

Jean-Claude Duvalier was born on July 3, 1951, in Port-au-Prince, Haiti. He graduated from secondary school in Port-au-Prince, and briefly attended law school at the University of Haiti. He succeeded his father as president for life in April 1971, becoming the youngest president in the world at age 19.

Partly because of pressure from the United States to moderate the tyrannical and corrupt practices of his father's regime, Duvalier instituted budgetary and judicial reforms, released some political prisoners, and eased press censorship, professing a policy of "gradual democratization of institutions." Nevertheless, no sharp changes from previous policies occurred. No political opposition was tolerated, and important political officials and judges were appointed by the president. Under Duvalier, Haiti continued a semi-isolationist approach to foreign relations, although the government actively solicited foreign aid to stimulate the economy.

In 1980 Duvalier married Michèle Bennett, who supplanted his hard-line mother, Simone, in Haitian politics. In the face of increasing social unrest, however, Duvalier and his wife left the country in February 1986, and a military council headed the country for several years. From 1986 Duvalier resided in France, despite the urging of Haitian authorities that he be extradited to stand trial for human rights abuses.

He returned to Haiti in January 2011, one year after the devastating 2010 earthquake. Two days later Duvalier was taken into custody by authorities for questioning regarding alleged corruption and embezzlement during his rule; he was subsequently released. He remained in Haiti but refused to appear for hearings on human rights violations he was alleged to have committed while president. In late February 2013 Duvalier was taken before a pretrial hearing to face questioning on those charges.

ELIZABETH I

(b. 1533–d. 1603)

Popularly known as the Virgin Queen and Good Queen Bess, Elizabeth Tudor became queen of England in 1558. The golden period of her reign is called the Elizabethan Age.

Elizabeth was born near London on September 7, 1533. Her father was Henry VIII. Her mother was Anne Boleyn, the second of Henry's six wives. Henry's first wife, Catherine of Aragon, had only one surviving child, Mary. Henry broke away from the Roman Catholic Church, annulled his marriage to Catherine and married Anne. Before Elizabeth was three years old, he had her mother beheaded.

Henry paid little attention to Elizabeth, but provided excellent tutors. She received the type of education normally reserved for male heirs, with a course of studies centering on classical languages, history, rhetoric, and moral philosophy.

Henry's third wife, Jane Seymour, gave birth to a son, Edward. Henry died when Edward was 10 years old, and the boy came to the throne as Edward VI. Elizabeth and Edward were both brought up in Henry's new church, called the Church of England. Their half sister Mary was brought up a Roman Catholic. When Edward died in

1553, Mary became queen and at once made Catholicism the state religion. Mary suspected Elizabeth of plotting with the Protestants to gain the throne and had her imprisoned in the Tower of London.

When Mary I died, there were two claimants to the English throne. If Elizabeth did not produce an heir, the next in line for the throne was her cousin Mary Stuart—the Catholic queen commonly known as Mary, Queen of Scots—who was about to be married to the dauphin Francis of France. If she won the throne of England, both Scotland and England would be joined to France. Philip II of Spain,

Portrait of Queen Elizabeth I of England, by artist Steven Van Der Meulen. Carl De Souza/ AFP/Getty Images

though a Catholic, threw his influence on the side of Elizabeth because he was jealous of France's power.

Elizabeth at age 25 had a genius for diplomacy, understood finance, and was extremely frugal in the expenses of government. She hated war because it was wasteful of both men and money. The young queen chose as her chief minister Sir William Cecil (Lord Burghley), who was cautious and conservative, like herself. For 40 years he was her mainstay in both home and foreign affairs.

Elizabeth's refusal to marry was the cause of great national and international discussion. The queen's marriage decision was critical not only for the question of succession but also for the tangled web of international diplomacy. Yet Elizabeth found maidenhood to be her most useful diplomatic weapon, particularly in playing the rivals France and Spain against each other. Among her prominent suitors was Philip II of Spain. She refused to marry him but held out hopes to more than one of his royal relatives when France seemed to threaten. Later, when Philip turned against England, Elizabeth encouraged French princes.

In religious matters, Elizabeth steered a middle course between the extreme Protestants (Puritans) and the Catholics. She restored the Protestant service but retained many features of Catholicism, including bishops and archbishops. The Catholics, who formed a majority of her subjects, were not reconciled by this compromise.

In 1568 Mary, having been forced to abdicate her Scottish throne, fled across the English border to ask for Elizabeth's help. Elizabeth kept her prisoner for 19 years. During this time Mary became involved in some of the plots against the queen. Finally, Mary was accused of having a part in a plot to assassinate Elizabeth, and she was beheaded in 1587.

During the first 30 years of Elizabeth's reign, commerce revived, and English ships were venturing overseas to the West Indies. There they came into conflict with Spain, which dominated the Caribbean region and claimed a monopoly of trade. Elizabeth aided the English seamen with ships and money.

King Philip II of Spain finally decided to put an end to these attacks by invading and conquering England. After years of preparation, Philip assembled a great fleet of his best and largest warships, called the "Armada." In 1588 the Armada sailed into the English Channel. In a nine-day battle the English inflicted terrible losses on the enemy, and finally won.

Elizabeth's reign is most often defined in terms of the religious question and the defeat of the Spanish Armada, but was also known for the flourishing of literature. The most splendid period of English literature, called the Elizabethan Age, began in the later years of Elizabeth's reign. Francis Bacon, writer of the *Essays*, was one of the queen's lawyers. Edmund Spenser wrote *The Faerie Queene* in her honor. William Shakespeare acted before her, but at the time of her death he had not yet written most of his great tragedies. Elizabeth enjoyed plays, but there is no evidence that she appreciated Shakespeare's genius.

Also important, were hundreds of laws on shipping, commerce, industry, currency reform, roads, relief for the poor, and agriculture. These laws shaped the policy of England for more than two centuries after Elizabeth's reign had ended.

Elizabeth died on March 24, 1603, at the age of 69. She was buried with great ceremony in Westminster Abbey.

CRISTINA FERNÁNDEZ DE KIRCHNER

(b. 1953–)

Argentinian lawyer and politician Cristina Fernández de Kirchner became the first female elected president of Argentina in 2007. She succeeded her husband, Néstor Kirchner, who had served as president from 2003 to 2007.

Cristina Fernández was born on Feb. 19, 1953, in La Plata, Argentina. She attended the National University of La Plata, where she met Kirchner, a fellow law student. In 1975 she and Kirchner married. One year later, after the military junta seized control of Argentina, the couple fled La Plata for Néstor's hometown of Río Gallegos. There they opened a law practice and, with the return of democracy in 1983, became active in electoral politics. Fernández de Kirchner was a provincial delegate to the Peronist party convention in 1985 and was later elected to the provincial legislature. Her husband won election as mayor of Río Gallegos in 1987, and in 1991 he was elected to the first of three consecutive four-year terms as provincial governor.

Fernández de Kirchner represented Santa Cruz in the Argentine Senate from 1995 to 1997 and from 2001 to 2005. She also served in the Chamber of Deputies from 1997 to 2001. During her tenure in Congress, she was one of the most vocal critics of the Peronist administration of Pres. Carlos Menem, voting frequently against his legislative initiatives. Her husband assumed the presidency in 2003 after Menem withdrew from the race.

In 2007 Kirchner decided not to run for reelection, and Fernández de Kirchner began campaigning for the presidency. She held a large lead in the polls and subsequently was elected president. In early 2008 she imposed a new tax system to increase export taxes on grains in an attempt to control Argentine food prices. Her actions were met with large-scale strikes and protests by farmers' unions throughout the country, which continued for four months and eventually resulted in food shortages. In order to regain control, Fernández de Kirchner agreed to submit the measure to Congress. The increase in taxes was approved by the Chamber of Deputies but was rejected by the Senate by one vote.

In Argentina's June 2009 legislative elections, Fernández de Kirchner suffered a major defeat when the ruling Peronist party lost power in both houses of Congress; her husband also lost his bid for a congressional seat and subsequently resigned as leader of the party. Néstor Kirchner passed away from heart failure in 2010 and was given a state funeral. After her husband's death, Kirchner staged a dramatic comeback in the 2011 elections, where she won the presidency with nearly 54 percent of the vote.

FRANCISCO FRANCO

(b. 1892–d. 1975)

Unlike many other modern dictators, Francisco Franco was soft-spoken and religious. He began his long reign as the dictator of Spain in 1939.

Franco was born on Dec. 4, 1892, in El Ferrol, Galicia, the northwestern-most province of Spain. His father, Nicholas, was a naval officer. His mother was Pilar Bahamonde. Franco entered the Military Academy at Toledo in 1907 and graduated in July 1910 as a second lieutenant. At 17 he was in Spanish Morocco fighting the Riffians. He rose in rank rapidly. He was a major at 23, commander of the Spanish foreign legion at 30, and a general at 34, the youngest in Europe at the time. After that Franco's fortunes rose and fell with the change of governments.

In July 1936 a carefully organized revolt against the government broke out. This revolt was to develop into the Spanish civil war. General José Sanjurjo, the chief conspirator against the republic, died suddenly shortly after the outbreak of the revolt. Franco then became leader of the rebels. In October he was named head of state and generalissimo of the army. In 1937 Franco abolished all political parties except the rebel Falange (Phalanx). He became its head and assumed the title El Caudillo (The Leader). Franco formed a cabinet in 1938 and became premier. On March 28, 1939, Franco's troops captured Madrid, and the civil war ended.

During World War II Franco switched his favor from side to side, depending upon whether the Axis powers or the Allies seemed to be winning. Secret documents released in 1946, however, revealed his close ties with the Axis and plans to enter the war.

In 1947 Spain was declared a kingdom. Franco was named chief of state for life and was given the right to choose his successor. Roman Catholicism was made the state religion. In 1973 Franco relinquished his role as premier of the Spanish government. He remained head of state, commander-in-chief of the armed forces, and leader of the Falange.

When Franco became ill in July 1974, and again in October 1975, his authority was transferred to Prince Juan Carlos de Bourbon. El Caudillo died in Madrid on Nov. 20, 1975.

INDIRA GANDHI

(b. 1917–d. 1984)

An aggressive fighter in the struggle for Indian independence, Indira Gandhi was the first woman prime minister of India. She was the only child of Jawaharlal Nehru, who became India's first prime minister.

She was born Indira Nehru on Nov. 19, 1917, in Allahabad, India. Her family was active in the nonviolent resistance movement led by Mahatma Gandhi against Great Britain's colonial rule of India. At the age of 12 she joined the movement by organizing thousands of Indian children to aid the adults who were working for independence.

Indira attended school in India and Switzerland. In 1934 she studied art and dancing at the university at Santiniketan. Later she attended Oxford University in England. In March 1942 she married Feroze Gandhi, a friend from her student days in England. A few months after their marriage, Indira Gandhi was arrested after she spoke at a public meeting in defiance of a British ban. She was imprisoned for thirteen months.

After India achieved independence in 1947, Indira toured refugee camps to aid victims of a Hindu-Muslim religious war. She accompanied her father on his official visits all over the world and campaigned for him during elections.

Beginning in 1959, Indira Gandhi served for a year as president of the Indian National Congress, the majority political party. She became the minister of information and broadcasting in the cabinet of Prime Minister Lal Bahadur Shastri, who succeeded Nehru after his death in May 1964.

When Shastri died in January 1966, Gandhi was elected prime minister by the Congress Party and won subsequent elections in 1967 and 1971. Her government faced crop failures and food riots, poverty, student unrest, and resistance from the many different language groups to the adoption of Hindi as the nation's official language. In 1971 Gandhi led India in a successful war against Pakistan to separate East and West Pakistan and establish the nation of Bangladesh.

In 1975 Gandhi was convicted on two counts of corruption in the 1971 campaign. While appealing the decision, she declared a state of emergency, imprisoned her political opponents, and assumed emergency powers. Governing by decree, she imposed total press censorship and implemented a policy of large-scale sterilization as a form of birth control. When long-postponed national elections were held in 1977, Gandhi and her party were soundly defeated.

Reelected to Parliament in 1978, Gandhi was soon expelled and jailed briefly. While misconduct charges were still pending, she campaigned as an activist who would curb inflation and crime. A landslide victory returned her to office in 1980. Faced with the problem of Sikh extremists in the Punjab using violence to assert their demands in an autonomous state, Gandhi ordered the Indian army on June 6, 1984, to storm the Golden Temple at Amritsar, the Sikhs' holiest shrine, which had been converted into an armory. Hundreds of Sikhs died in the attack.

Five months later, on Oct. 31, 1984, Gandhi was killed in her garden by bullets fired by two of her own Sikh bodyguards. The assassination was widely believed to be revenge for the attack on the Golden Temple.

MOHANDAS KARAMCHAND GANDHI

(b. 1869–d. 1948)

Throughout history, most national heroes have been warriors, but Gandhi ended British rule over his native India without striking a single blow. A gentle and devout man, he nonetheless had an iron will; nothing could change his convictions. This combination of traits made him the leader of India's nationalist movement. Some observers called him a master politician. Others believed him a saint. To millions of Hindus he was their beloved Mahatma, meaning "great soul."

Mohandas Karamchand Gandhi was born on Oct. 2, 1869, in Porbandar, near Bombay. His father had been prime minister of several small native states. Gandhi was married when he was only 13 years old.

When he was 19 he defied custom by going abroad to study. He studied law at University College in London. Fellow students snubbed him because he was an Indian. In his lonely hours he studied philosophy and he discovered the principle of nonviolence as evident in Henry David Thoreau's *Civil Disobedience*. He was persuaded by John Ruskin's plea to give up industrialism for farm life and traditional handicrafts—ideals similar to many Hindu religious ideas.

In 1891 Gandhi returned to India, and went to South Africa in 1893. At Natal he was the first so-called "colored" lawyer admitted to the Supreme Court. His interest soon turned to the problem of fellow Indians who had come to South Africa as laborers. He had seen how they were treated as inferiors in India, in England, and then in South Africa. In 1894 he founded the Natal Indian Congress to agitate for Indian rights. Yet he remained loyal to the British Empire.

Later in 1906, however, Gandhi began his peaceful revolution. He declared he would go to jail or even die before obeying an anti-Asian law. Thousands of Indians joined him in this civil disobedience campaign. He was imprisoned twice. Yet in World War I he again organized an ambulance corps for the British before returning home to India in 1914.

Gandhi's writings and devout life won him a mass of Indian followers. They followed him almost blindly in his campaign for *swaraj*, or "home rule." He worked to reconcile all classes and religious sects, especially Hindus and Muslims. In 1919 he became a leader in the newly formed Indian National Congress political party. In 1920 he launched a noncooperation campaign against Britain, urging Indians to spin their own cotton and to boycott British goods, courts, and government. This led to his imprisonment from 1922 to 1924. In 1930, in protest of a salt

Mahatma Gandhi (center, holding a staff), arriving in Simla, the capital of the Indian state Himachal Pradesh, to meet with local officials. Fox Photos/ Hulton Archive/Getty Images

tax, Gandhi led thousands of Indians on a 200-mile (320-kilometer) march to the sea to collect their own salt. Again he was jailed.

In 1934 he retired as head of the party but remained its actual leader. Gradually he became convinced that India would receive no real freedom as long as it remained in the British Empire. Early in World War II he demanded immediate independence as India's price for aiding Britain in the war. He was imprisoned for the third time, from 1942 to 1944.

Gandhi's victory came in 1947 when India won independence. The subcontinent split into two countries (India and Pakistan) and brought Hindu-Muslim riots. Again Gandhi turned to nonviolence, fasting until Delhi rioters pledged peace to him. On Jan. 30, 1948, while on his way to prayer in Delhi, Gandhi was killed by a Hindu who had been maddened by the Mahatma's efforts to reconcile Hindus and Muslims.

GIUSEPPE GARIBALDI

(b. 1807–d. 1882)

When Italian patriot and soldier Garibaldi was born, there was no Italy, only a group of small backward states. These states had long been under foreign domination. Garibaldi was one of the three great leaders who freed the Italians from foreign rule and unified the country.

Giuseppe Garibaldi was born in Nice on July 4, 1807. His father was a fisherman. In search of a life of adventure, the boy went to sea. He was in the navy of the kingdom of Piedmont-Sardinia when he joined Young Italy, a secret society of young men that was formed by Giuseppe Mazzini to drive Austria from Italy and to unify the peninsula.

In 1834 Garibaldi plotted to seize the frigate on which he was sailing to help in the freeing of Genoa. The plot was discovered, but he escaped. He made his way to South America. There he took part in wars, first in Brazil and then in Uruguay, where he raised and commanded the Italian Legion. He also met the daring Anna Maria Ribeiro da Silva (called Anita), whom he married in 1842.

Revolution and insurrection raged throughout the Italian peninsula in 1848. Garibaldi returned, a master of guerrilla warfare, and was hailed as the "hero of Montevideo." He raised volunteers and was given command of the forces of the short-lived Roman Republic, which Mazzini had set up. After a desperate defense he was forced to flee with his followers across the peninsula, pursued by the Austrians. Once more Garibaldi became an exile. For a time he worked as a candle maker in New York City.

Returning to Italy in 1854, Garibaldi settled down on the small island of Caprera. In 1859 war broke out anew with Austria. After fighting in the Alps, Garibaldi decided to aid the Sicilians, who had revolted against their king, Francis II of Naples. In May 1860 his thousand "red shirts" on two small steamers reached the island. He took Sicily in the name of Victor Emmanuel II.

Thousands of volunteers rushed to join Garibaldi's army. In August he crossed to the mainland to march on Naples. When he entered the city, crowds sang the popular national anthem, now called "Garibaldi's Hymn." After turning over the city to Victor Emmanuel II, Garibaldi returned to his humble life on Caprera. On Feb. 18, 1861, the kingdom of Italy was finally proclaimed.

Garibaldi was determined to seize Rome, which was still under the rule of the pope. This would have brought both France and

Austria against Italy. Twice the Italian government was forced to take the radical Garibaldi prisoner. When Italian troops finally did enter Rome, in 1870, he had no part in the triumph. He was helping the French Republic in the Franco-Prussian War. When the Franco-Prussian War was over, Garibaldi retired once more, on a generous pension, to Caprera. There he spent the rest of his life, dying on June 2, 1882.

CHARLES DE GAULLE

(b. 1890–d. 1970)

Twice in 20 years France looked to Charles de Gaulle for leadership in a time of trouble. General de Gaulle led the Free French government in the dark days of World War II. In 1958 he returned to power as president in an attempt to save France from civil war.

Charles-André-Joseph-Marie de Gaulle was born on Nov. 22, 1890, at Lille, in northern France. His father was a philosophy professor. His mother was a descendant of Scottish and Irish refugees who had fled to France.

In 1911 de Gaulle graduated near the head of his class from the prestigious military school at St-Cyr and became a second lieutenant in the infantry. At the Battle of Verdun in 1916 he was captured by the Germans. De Gaulle made five unsuccessful attempts to escape. He was released after the 1918 armistice. In 1921 de Gaulle married Yvonne Vendroux; they had three children.

After World War I de Gaulle served on a military mission to Poland and then taught military history at St-Cyr. He served in the army in Germany and the Middle East. He also wrote *The Army of the Future* (1934), in which he was one of the first to suggest the use of a professional, mechanized infantry.

When Germany invaded France in 1940, de Gaulle was made a brigadier general and given command of an armored division. France failed to check the German advance, and signed a truce with Adolf Hitler. De Gaulle flew to London for a series of conferences with British Prime Minister Winston Churchill. From his London base, he took control of the newly formed Free French resistance movement. After the American invasion of North Africa he joined Gen. Henri Giraud in Algiers to serve as copresident of the French Committee of National Liberation. De Gaulle later became sole president of the committee and chief of the Free French armed forces. He returned to Paris in 1944 on the heels of the retreating Germans.

Appointed president of the newly established French provisional government, de Gaulle tried to unite France's many political parties into a strong national administration. De Gaulle had always been opposed to France's historic system of an all-powerful legislature. He advocated a strong presidency as a check on the National Assembly. De Gaulle's proposed constitutional reforms met with increasing hostility from the Assembly, and early in 1946 he resigned.

In 1947, still working for a strong central government, he organized a new political party—the Rally of the French People. In the years that followed, de Gaulle's warnings against unstable government were justified. No French government was able to stay in power for more than a few months. A major cause of the political uproar was the civil war fought in Algeria over French attempts to preserve colonialism in North Africa.

In 1958 de Gaulle went to Paris for an interview with President René Coty, who asked him to try to form a new government. De Gaulle agreed but only if the National Assembly would vote him the executive powers that he had long sought. France's Fifth Republic was formed in December, and de Gaulle took office as its first president on Jan. 8, 1959.

De Gaulle promoted peace negotiations in Algeria. In a nationwide referendum, the voters of France overwhelmingly supported a cease-fire agreement he had announced in March 1962. De Gaulle declared Algeria's independence on July 3.

In the 1960s de Gaulle increased his efforts to make France a leading world power. At his urging the French developed a nuclear force and a space program. In international affairs de Gaulle rejected the nuclear test ban treaty; blocked the United Kingdom's entry into the European Economic Community, or Common Market; and formally recognized Communist China.

After a runoff election, de Gaulle was inaugurated president for a second seven-year term in January 1966. Later in the year he ended

French participation in the military activities of the North Atlantic Treaty Organization (NATO).

In 1969 de Gaulle again demanded a vote of confidence when he submitted a number of constitutional changes to a national referendum. On April 27 the people of France voted down his proposals. The following day de Gaulle submitted his resignation and retired to his home at Colombey-les-Deux-Églises, where he died on Nov. 9, 1970. A memorial Cross of Lorraine was erected near his grave in 1972.

GENGHIS KHAN

(b. 1162?–d. 1227)

A statue of Genghis Khan on horseback dwarfs a Mongolian museum dedicated to the warrior and leader. Peter Zachar/Shutterstock.com

From the high, windswept Gobi came one of history's most famous warriors. He was a Mongolian nomad known as Genghis Khan. With his fierce, hard-riding nomad horde, he conquered a huge empire that stretched through Asia from the Yellow Sea to the Black Sea.

Genghis Khan was born on the Gobi, in a yurt, or felt tent, on a bank of the Onon River in northern Mongolia. His father, Yesügei, was the chief of several desert tribes and had just slain a foe named Temüjin. In triumph Yesügei named his newborn son Temüjin.

Yesügei died when Temüjin was nine years old. The boy succeeded him, but the fierce, restless nomads would not obey so young a chieftain. The chief of another tribe proclaimed himself leader of the Mongols and captured Temüjin. Guards forced Temüjin into a *kang*, a wooden yoke that shackled his shoulders and wrists. In the dark he slowly twisted himself to reach above a guard and smashed the *kang* down on his head. Then Temüjin raced to the river and escaped by hiding in water up to his chin.

Temüjin's bold courage and resourcefulness began to win followers. When he reached manhood, he conquered the Tatars and added them to his tribes. In 1203 he defeated the Keraits. Seizing their cities of mud and stone, he made Karakorum his capital.

In 1206 a council of his tribes named him Genghis Khan. It means "greatest of rulers, emperor of all men." Genghis Khan then put his Mongolian realm under Yassa, a body of laws he assembled from various tribal codes. These laws demanded obedience to Genghis Khan, unity of the tribes, and pitiless punishment of wrongdoers. Through Yassa, Genghis Khan achieved the discipline that welded his wild tribesmen into merciless, successful armies.

On his march of conquest Genghis Khan overran North China from 1208 to 1215. Wheeling westward, his horde conquered Turkestan. Then his armies engulfed neighboring countries, even part of India. In 1222 the Mongols struck into Europe at the Don River. After defeating the Russians, they pushed to the Dnieper River. Victorious, Genghis Khan returned eastward. At his death his empire passed to his sons.

GERONIMO

(b. 1829–d. 1909)

A formidable leader of the Chiricahua Apache in the defense of their homeland against the invasion of white settlers, Geronimo today is considered a genuine legend of the Old West. Embittered at the slaughter and displacement of his people, he displayed exceptional courage and skill in leading attacks on both the Mexican and the U.S. military. His ceaseless efforts brought great turmoil and bloodshed to east-central Arizona, however, and Geronimo and his followers ultimately were outmatched by thousands of well-armed U.S. troops.

Geronimo was born in June 1829 in No-Doyohn Canyon, which is located somewhere in what is now southeastern Arizona or southwestern New Mexico. His Apache name was Goyathlay, which means "one who yawns." After he was admitted to the tribal warriors' council in 1846, the young Geronimo participated in numerous raids in northern Mexico. The murders of his mother, wife, and children at the hands of the Mexican military in 1858 galvanized the young warrior into a position of leadership.

Geronimo inherited a generations-old tradition of resisting colonization by both Spaniards and North Americans. In 1874 about 4,000 Apaches were forcibly moved to a barren wasteland called the San Carlos reservation in Arizona. They looked to Geronimo, who led them into a period of armed resistance that lasted, with interruptions, until his final surrender in September 1886.

After his surrender Geronimo never saw Arizona again in spite of promises made at the time. Along with other captured Native Americans, he was put to work doing hard labor in Florida. He was finally settled at Fort Sill, Okla., in 1894, where he tried to farm and joined the Dutch Reformed Church. His continued participation in local gambling led to his expulsion from the church, however. The War Department granted him special permission to sell photographs of himself and his handiwork at expositions. He died at Fort Sill on Feb. 17, 1909. His dictated autobiography, *Geronimo: His Own Story*, was published in 1906.

MIKHAIL GORBACHEV

(b. 1931–)

At the age of 54, Mikhail Gorbachev became the youngest man to head the government of the Soviet Union since Joseph Stalin came to power in the 1920s. Gorbachev was also the first general secretary of the Communist Party not to have served in the armed forces during World War II.

Mikhail Sergeevich Gorbachev was born on March 2, 1931, at Privolnoye in the Stavropol territory of the Soviet Union. He studied law at Moscow State University and joined the Communist Party in 1952. After graduation he joined the Komsomol, the Young Communist League, and rose steadily in party organizations.

In 1971 Gorbachev was elected to the Central Committee of the party, and he was appointed secretary for agriculture in 1978. He was made a full member of the Politburo, the governing body of the Soviet Union, in 1980. He was its youngest member. In 1988 Gorbachev became Soviet president and chief of state.

Shortly after taking office in 1985, Gorbachev initiated a series of policies

Soviet President Mikhail Gorbachev, during a 1990 debate on economic reform in Moscow. Vitaly Armand/AFP/Getty Images

aimed at a complete restructuring of Soviet society. The terms *glasnost* (openness) and *perestroika* (restructuring) came into common use as he tried to undo 70 years of economic stagnation and political repression. Through a restructuring of the constitution and open elections he also brought a measure of democracy to Soviet politics. It became evident within a few years that Gorbachev's goal was to combine reform with retention of a modified Communist system. As a democratic movement grew, however, opponents insisted that Communism had proved totally unworkable. They demanded the adoption of a free-market economy, a step Gorbachev was unwilling to take.

Gorbachev gained some stunning triumphs in foreign policy. He withdrew all Soviet troops from Afghanistan by early 1989. He also began troop reductions in Eastern Europe. He and President Ronald

Reagan signed the Intermediate-Range Nuclear Forces (INF) treaty on Dec. 8, 1987, in Washington, D.C. Gorbachev and President George Bush held summits in 1989 and 1990.

Gorbachev's bold foreign policy actions, added to his encouragement of democracy in the Soviet Union, had a completely unintended consequence: the collapse of Communism in Eastern Europe in 1989. Gorbachev was named the 1990 winner of the Nobel Prize for Peace. The first Communist head of state to be so honored, he was recognized for promoting the political changes in Eastern Europe and for ending the Cold War.

Despite his popularity outside the Soviet Union, Gorbachev faced serious problems at home by 1990 because of a worsening economy. He was proving himself a reluctant reformer and was challenged by a democratic movement headed by Boris Yeltsin, president of the Russian Republic. At the same time, old-line Communists opposed reform. On Aug. 19, 1991, they staged a coup to remove Gorbachev from power. Yeltsin, however, rallied the people, and the coup failed within 72 hours. By then Yeltsin had become the leading power in the country. The Communist Party was banned. The Baltic States received their independence in September. By December the Soviet Union itself had come apart. Eleven of the remaining former republics formed the Commonwealth of Independent States. Gorbachev, with no nation to rule, resigned his office on December 25 and went into retirement.

HAILE SELASSIE

(b. 1892–d. 1975)

W hen Haile Selassie came to the throne of Ethiopia, he was a progressive ruler and the hope of young moderates hoping to modernize their country. By the end of his reign he had become a virtual dictator, overthrowing the old constitution and taking all power into his own hands.

Haile Selassie was born Tafari Makonnen on July 23, 1892, near Harar, Ethiopia. His father was right-hand man to Emperor Menelik II, and he was quickly given the responsibilities of a young nobleman. By 1910 he was governor of his native province. When the emperor's daughter Zauditu became empress in 1916, Tafari was named regent and heir to the throne. In 1923 he brought Ethiopia into the League of Nations, and in 1924 he visited Europe—the first ruler of Ethiopia to travel abroad

He assumed the title of king in 1928, and upon Zauditu's death in 1930 he had himself proclaimed emperor as Haile Selassie. The name means "might of the trinity." Ethiopia was a Christian nation, and the emperor was supposedly descended from ancient Israel's King Solomon. Another of his numerous titles was Lion of Judah. In 1931 a new constitution greatly limited the powers of the parliament and within a few years it had become defunct.

His rule was interrupted in 1935 by Italy's invasion of Ethiopia, which forced him into exile. He returned in 1941 when British and Ethiopian troops recaptured the capital. Although restored as emperor, he had to re-create the authority he had once held. In 1955 he issued a new constitution, giving himself all governing authority. Except for an army revolt in December 1960, Haile Selassie ruled with little opposition until 1974, when he was deposed by a provisional military government. He died under uncertain circumstances, a captive in his own palace, on Aug. 27, 1975.

DAG HAMMARSKJÖLD

(b. 1905–d. 1961)

Swedish economist and statesman Dag Hammarskjöld served as the second secretary-general of the United Nations (UN). He is credited with helping develop the UN into an effective and respected international organization. Hammarskjöld was posthumously awarded the Nobel Prize for Peace in 1961.

Dag Hjalmar Agne Carl Hammarskjöld was born on July 29, 1905, in Jönköping, Sweden. He was the son of Hjalmar Hammarskjöld, the prime minister of Sweden from 1914 to 1917. Hammarskjöld studied law and economics at the universities of Uppsala and Stockholm and taught political economy at Stockholm from 1933 to 1936. He then joined the Swedish civil service as permanent undersecretary in the Ministry of

Finance and subsequently became president of the board of the Bank of Sweden. From 1947 he served in the Ministry of Foreign Affairs.

In 1951 Hammarskjöld was chosen vice chairman of Sweden's delegation to the UN General Assembly, of which he became chairman in 1952. On April 10, 1953, five months after the resignation of Trygve Lie of Norway as secretary-general, Hammarskjöld was elected to the office for a term of five years. The absence of a major international crisis during the first three years of his secretary-ship enabled him to concentrate on quietly building public confidence in himself and his office. In September 1957 he was reelected to another five-year term.

As secretary-general, Hammarskjöld faced a number of daunting challenges in the Middle East and Africa. He and Canadian statesman Lester Pearson participated in the resolution of the Suez Canal crisis that arose in 1956. Hammarskjöld also played a prominent role in resolving crises in Lebanon and Jordan in 1958. After the Belgian Congo became the independent Republic of the Congo (now Democratic Republic of the Congo) on June 30, 1960, Hammarskjöld sent a UN force there to suppress the civil strife that followed. While on a peace mission to President Moise Tshombe of the secessionist Congolese province of Katanga, Hammarskjöld was killed in an airplane crash.

VÁCLAV HAVEL

(b. 1936–d. 2011)

Václav Havel began his professional life as a playwright and poet. Havel was drawn into politics and, in 1989, he became the first non-Communist leader of Czechoslovakia in forty years.

Havel was born on Oct. 5, 1936, in Prague, Czechoslovakia (now Czech Republic). He was the son of a wealthy restaurateur whose property was confiscated by the Communist government of Czechoslovakia in 1948. As the son of bourgeois (middle class) parents, Havel was denied easy access to education but managed to finish high school and study on the university level. He found work as a stagehand in a Prague theatrical company in 1959 and soon began writing plays. By 1968 Havel had progressed to the position of resident playwright of the Theatre of the Balustrade company.

Havel was a prominent participant in the liberal reforms of 1968 (known as the Prague Spring), and, after the Soviet clampdown on Czechoslovakia that year, his plays were banned and his passport was confiscated. During the 1970s and '80s he was repeatedly arrested and served four years in prison (1979–83) for his activities on behalf of human rights in Czechoslovakia. After his release from prison Havel remained in his homeland.

Havel continued to write plays steadily until the late 1980s. When massive antigovernment demonstrations erupted in Prague in November 1989, Havel became the leading figure in the Civic Forum, a new coalition of noncommunist opposition groups pressing for democratic reforms. In early December the Communist Party capitulated and formed a coalition government with the Civic Forum. As a result of an agreement between the partners in this bloodless "Velvet Revolution," Havel was elected to the post of interim president of Czechoslovakia on December 29, 1989, and he was reelected to the presidency in July 1990, becoming the country's first noncommunist leader since 1948.

As the Czechoslovak union faced dissolution in 1992, Havel, who opposed the division, resigned from office. The following year he was elected president of the new Czech Republic. His political role, however, was limited, as Prime Minister Václav Klaus commanded much of the power. In 1998 Havel was reelected by a narrow margin, and, under his presidency, the Czech Republic joined the North Atlantic Treaty Organization (NATO) in 1999.

Barred constitutionally from seeking a third term, Havel stepped down as president in 2003. He died Dec. 18, 2011, in the Czech Republic city of Hrádeček.

HENRY VIII

(b. 1491–d. 1547)

Reigning from 1509 to 1547, Henry VIII was one of England's strongest and least popular monarchs. He is remembered for his six wives and his quarrel with the Roman Catholic Church, which led to the creation of the Church of England.

Henry was born in Greenwich, near London, on June 28, 1491. He was the second son of Henry VII, the first of the Tudor line of kings, and Elizabeth, daughter of Edward IV, first king of the short-lived line of York. The first English ruler to be educated under the influence of the Renaissance, he was a gifted scholar, linguist, composer, and musician. He succeeded his father on the throne in 1509, and soon thereafter married his elder brother's Arthur's young widow, Catherine of Aragon.

During the first 20 years of his reign, he left the shaping of policies largely in the hands of his great counselor, Cardinal Wolsey. By 1527 Henry had made up his mind to get rid of his wife. Only one of Catherine's six children, the sickly princess Mary survived infancy, and it was doubtful whether a woman could succeed to the English throne. Then too, Henry had fallen in love with a lady of the court, Anne Boleyn. When Pope Clement VII would not annul his marriage, Henry held Wolsey responsible and turned against him. The king deprived Wolsey of the office of chancellor and had him arrested on a charge of treason. In 1533 Henry obtained a divorce through Thomas Cranmer, whom he had made archbishop of Canterbury, and it was soon announced that Henry had married Anne Boleyn.

The pope was thus defied. Under the leadership of Thomas Cromwell, who had become the king's principal adviser in 1532, all ties that bound the English church to Rome were broken. All payments to Rome were stopped, and the pope's authority in England was abolished. In 1534 the Act of Supremacy declared Henry himself to be Supreme Head of the Church of England, and anyone who denied this title was guilty of an act of treason.

The Bible was translated into English, and printed copies were placed in the churches. The monasteries throughout England were dissolved and their vast lands and goods turned over to the king, who in turn granted those estates to noblemen who would support his policies. The result was a great expansion of Henry's power.

Although Henry reformed the government of the church, he refused to allow any changes to be made in its doctrines. After the separation from Rome he persecuted with equal severity the Catholics who adhered to the government of Rome and the Protestants who rejected its doctrines.

Henry was married six times. Anne Boleyn bore the king one child, who became Elizabeth I. Henry soon tired of Anne and had her put to death. A few days later he married a third wife, Jane Seymour. She died a little later, after having given birth to the future Edward VI. A marriage was then contracted with a German princess, Anne of Cleves. The king had been led to believe that she was very beautiful. When he discovered that he had been tricked, he promptly divorced her and beheaded Thomas Cromwell, who had arranged the marriage. Henry's fifth wife, Catherine Howard, was sent to the block for misconduct. In 1543 he married his sixth wife, the tactful and pious Catherine Parr.

Although he himself opposed the Protestant Reformation, his creation of a national church marked the real beginning of the English Reformation. Henry died on January 28, 1547, and was buried in St. George's Chapel in Windsor Castle.

HIROHITO

(b. 1901–d. 1989)

Tradition says that Hirohito, the longest-reigning monarch of modern times, was the 124th direct descendant of the fabled first emperor, Jimmu, and therefore a member of the oldest imperial family in the world. In Japan he was considered sacred and referred to as Tenno Heika, meaning "son of heaven." So significant is the role of the emperor in Japanese society that, when Japan surrendered in World War II, he was allowed to retain his position and title.

Michinomiya Hirohito was born at Aoyama Palace in Tokyo on April 29, 1901. He received his early education at the Peers' School and later attended the Crown Prince's Institute. He studied marine biology, on which he later wrote several books based on research he had done in Sagami Bay. In 1921 he paid a visit to Europe, the first Japanese crown prince to do so. When he returned home he was named prince regent to rule in place of his father, who had retired because of mental illness.

Japanese Emperor Hirohito and his wife, Nagakute, following a vote on Japan's postwar constitution in 1946. AFP/Getty Images

The first 20 years of Hirohito's reign were tumultuous. By the time he became emperor in 1926, following the death of his father, the military was already in firm control of policy and impelling Japan into a major war.

There has been considerable debate among historians about the role Hirohito played during Japan's militaristic period from the early 1930s to 1945, the end of World War II. Many have asserted that he had grave misgivings about war with the United States and was opposed to Japan's alliance with Germany and Italy but that he was constrained to go along with the militarists who increasingly came to dominate the armed forces and the government. Other historians have claimed that Hirohito was actively involved in the planning of Japan's expansionist policies from the Japanese invasion of Manchuria in 1931 to the end of the war. Still others posit that the truth lies somewhere between those two interpretations.

In 1945, when Japan was nearing defeat, opinion was divided between those who favored surrender and those who wanted to carry on the war to the bitter end. Hirohito sided with those urging peace. On Aug. 15, 1945, he broadcast on radio his country's surrender.

After the war, there were changes in Hirohito's position. He renounced his divinity. The constitution that had given the emperor supreme authority was rewritten. The new constitution vested sovereignty in the people, and the emperor was designated "symbol of the

State and of the unity of the people." He became more accessible, making personal appearances and permitting publication of pictures and stories of himself and his family. In 1959 he permitted his son, Crown Prince Akihito, to marry a commoner.

Hirohito died on Jan. 7, 1989, after a long illness. Upon his death Prince Akihito automatically became emperor.

ADOLF HITLER

(b. 1889–d. 1945)

The rise of Adolf Hitler to the position of dictator of Germany is the story of a frenzied ambition that plunged the world into the worst war in history. Only an army corporal in World War I, Hitler became Germany's chancellor 15 years later.

Hitler was born on April 20, 1889, in Braunau-am-Inn, Austria, of German descent. His father, a petty customs official, wanted the boy to study for a government position. Meanwhile, the boy filled most of his school hours with daydreams of becoming a painter. His one school interest was history, especially that of the Germans.

Adolf Hitler, addressing the crowd at a rally.
Universal Images Group/Getty Images

Failure dogged him. After his father's death, when Adolf was 13, he studied watercolor painting, but accomplished little. After his mother's death, he went to Vienna but was rejected as untalented by the Academy of Arts there.

In 1912 Hitler left Vienna for Munich. At the outbreak of World War I in 1914, he gave up his Austrian citizenship to enlist in the 16th Bavarian infantry regiment. On the Somme in 1916 he was a "front fighter" against British tanks, rose to lance corporal, and won the Iron Cross as dispatch runner. In 1917 he fought in the third Battle of Ypres.

The armistice found him in a hospital, temporarily blinded by mustard gas and suffering from shock. No longer an Austrian citizen and not yet a German citizen, Hitler, at the war's end, was a man without a country. He remained in the army, stationed in Munich.

In the political and economic tempest that swept defeated Germany, Munich became a storm center. Officers of the beaten Reichswehr (German army) conspired to win control of Germany. They maintained "informers," one of whom was Hitler. He was assigned to report on "subversive activities" in Munich's political parties. This political spying was the turning point of Hitler's life.

In 1919 he joined the German Workers' Party, and soon took the lead. In 1920 Hitler changed the division's name to Nationalsozialistische Deutsche Arbeiterpartei (National Socialist German Workers' Party), abbreviated to Nazi. Hitler's voice, torn and hoarsened by mustard gas, was a hypnotic one. His speeches kindled the anger of rivals, especially the Communists, and they tried to break up his meetings. They were prevented from doing so by the brutal Nazis.

By 1923 the Nazis had grown strong enough in Munich to try to seize the government. The attempt failed and Hitler was convicted of treason, sentenced to five years that was later commuted to eight months. Emerging from prison in 1924, Hitler once again seemed destined to failure. The government had banned the Nazi Party, and only a handful of the members clung together. At length, however, Hitler was spurred back into a position of leadership.

From 1925 to 1927 Hitler was even forbidden to speak publicly in either Bavaria or Saxony. Then a world-wide depression plunged Germany again into poverty and unemployment, and the Nazis began to gain votes. By 1930 Hitler had the support of many industrialists and the military caste. In 1933 President Paul von Hindenburg appointed him chancellor.

Believing himself on the road to world conquest, in 1941 Hitler made himself Personal Commander of the Army and, in 1942, Supreme War Lord. Nazi propaganda had made Hitler a symbol of strength and national virtue. He had won German citizenship in 1930 only by the scheming of Nazi henchmen, yet he was hailed as the ideal German leader.

In November 1937, at a secret meeting of his military leaders, Hitler outlined his plans for future conquest, beginning with Austria and Czechoslovakia). In January 1938 he dispensed with the services of those who were not wholehearted in their acceptance of Nazi dynamism. He ordered the invasion of Austria by German troops, then proceeded to invade Czechoslovakia and Poland. The latter move was followed two days later by a British and French declaration of war on Germany. World War II had begun.

Covering his unsavory and cruel character, propaganda built a legend around Hitler by emphasizing his habits of self-denial and discipline, as well as what was considered his selfless devotion to Germany. Some of this legend vanished when his long, secret association with Eva Braun was revealed. He married her near the war's end, in April 1945, just before he committed suicide. Hitler was declared dead officially Oct. 25, 1956, after his remains had been definitely identified.

HO CHI MINH

(b. 1890–d. 1969)

As founder of the Indo-Chinese Communist Party in 1930 and president of North Vietnam from 1945 to 1969, Ho Chi Minh led the longest and most costly 20th-century war against colonialism. His whole adult life was devoted to ending French and, later, American domination of Vietnam. His goals were achieved in 1975, six years after his death, when the last Americans left South Vietnam.

Ho was born Nguyen Tat Thanh on May 19, 1890, in Hoang Tru, Vietnam (then known in the West as French Indochina). He attended school in Hue during his teen years, worked as a schoolmaster for a time, and went to a technical school in Saigon. In 1911 he went to work on ocean freighters, which took him around Africa and as far as Boston and New York City. After two years in London (1915–17) he moved to Paris and remained there until 1923. While in Paris he became a socialist and organized a group of Vietnamese living there in a protest against French colonial policy.

Inspired by the successful Communist revolution in Russia, he went to Moscow in 1924 and took part in the fifth Congress of the Communist International. His anticolonial views kept him from returning to Vietnam until the end of World War II. Much of his time was spent in China, where he organized the Indo-Chinese Communist Party on Feb. 3, 1930. It was in about 1940 that he began to use the name Ho Chi Minh, meaning "he who enlightens."

In 1941 Ho and his comrades formed the League for the Independence of Vietnam, or Vietminh. By 1945 the Japanese had overrun Vietnam and defeated the French, and later in the year the Japanese were defeated by the United States. Ho immediately sought the cooperation of the United States in preventing the return of colonial rule, and on Sept. 2, 1945, he proclaimed the independence of Vietnam.

This proclamation was premature: two Indochina wars were fought before Vietnam became independent. Ho's main contribution during the wars was keeping both the Soviet Union and China from gaining too great an influence in Vietnam. Although his death was reported on Sept. 3, 1969, in Hanoi, the Vietnamese Communist Party disclosed in 1989 that Ho had actually died on September 2, Vietnam's National Day.

HONGWU

(b. 1328–1398)

Hongwu was the reign name (*nianhao*) of the Chinese emperor (reigned 1368–98) who founded the Ming dynasty that ruled

China for nearly 300 years. During his reign, the Hongwu emperor instituted military, administrative, and educational reforms that centered power in the emperor.

The future Hongwu emperor was born in 1328 as Zhu Chongba, a poor peasant of Haozhou (about 100 miles [160 km] northwest of Nanjing, near China's east coast). Orphaned at 16, he became a monk to avoid starvation. As a wandering mendicant, he often begged for food at Hefei (some 100 miles west of Nanjing). More than seven million people starved as a result of drought and famine, a situation that encouraged the popular rebellions that started from around 1325. Led by plebeian bandits, the rebels attacked the rich, distributing their wealth and goods among the people.

One such rebel was Guo Zixing, who in 1352 led a large force to attack and take Haozhou. Zhu joined the rebel forces and changed his name to Zhu Yuanzhang, rising from the ranks to become second-in-command. In 1353 Zhu Yuanzhang captured Chuzhou (now in Anhui province, northwest of Nanjing). In 1355 Guo Zixing died, and Zhu Yuanzhang took over the leadership of the rebel army. Zhu Yuangzhang attacked and captured towns and cities in eastern China and, on reaching the Yangtze River (Chang Jiang) delta, encountered educated men of the gentry class. Some decided to join his movement, and Zhu had the foresight to seek their guidance. He was persuaded by his scholars to present himself as a national leader against the Mongols rather than as a popular rebel.

Now determined to overthrow the Yuan (Mongol) dynasty (1206–1368), Zhu marched toward Nanjing and captured it in 1356. Proclaiming himself Duke of Wu, Zhu established an effective administration over the Nanjing area. He also encouraged agriculture by granting unused land to the landless peasants, but, in spite of his successes, he was still reluctant to proclaim himself king (*wang*). At that time he acknowledged the Song dynasty pretender, Han Lin'er, as his superior, even though Han was ineffectual.

Zhu now emerged as the national leader against the Mongols, though he had other rivals for power. In 1367 the Song pretender Han Lin'er felt so threatened by the Mongols at his headquarters at Chuzhou that he decided to flee to Nanjing for protection. Han drowned when his boat capsized.

With the south pacified, Zhu sent his generals to lead troops against the north. At the beginning of 1368 Zhu finally proclaimed himself emperor of the Ming dynasty, establishing his capital at Nanjing. Hongwu ("vastly martial") was adopted as his reign title, and he is usually referred to as the Hongwu emperor, though Taizu is more strictly correct.

The Hongwu emperor was cruel, suspicious, and irrational, especially as he grew older. Instead of eliminating Mongol influence, he made his court resemble the Mongol court, and the despotic power of the emperor was institutionalized for the rest of the dynasty.

The trend toward political despotism can be seen in the Hongwu emperor's various other actions. In 1380 Prime Minister Hu Weiyong was implicated in a widespread plot to overthrow the throne and was executed along with 30,000 members of his clique.

The Hongwu emperor felt that, after the Mongol expulsion, the scholars formed the most dangerous group. Nevertheless, his interest in restoring traditional Chinese values involved rehabilitating the Confucian scholar class, and from experience he knew that effective government depended upon the scholars. He therefore encouraged education and purposely trained scholars for the bureaucracy. At the same time he used methods to deprive them of power and position.

In foreign relations the Hongwu emperor extended the Ming empire's prestige to outlying regions: southern Manchuria was brought into the empire; outlying states, such as Korea, the Liuqiu (i.e., Ryukyu) Islands, Annam, and other states, sent tribute missions to acknowledge the suzerainty of the Ming emperor; and, not satisfied with the expulsion of the Mongols, he sent two military expeditions into Mongolia, reaching the Mongol capital of Karakorum itself. When Ming emissaries traversed the mountains to Samarkand, however, they were met with a different reception. Timur (one of history's greatest conquerors) was building a new Mongol empire in that region, and the Chinese envoys were imprisoned. Eventually, they were released, and Timur and the Ming exchanged several embassies, which the Chinese regarded as tributary missions.

A great problem for the Hongwu emperor was the succession. In 1392, when the heir designate Yiwen died, the Hongwu emperor was persuaded to appoint Yiwen's eldest son as his successor, rather than his fourth son prince of Yan, who was angered by this decision. After the Hongwu emperor's death in June 1398, he was succeeded by his grandson Yunwen.

IBN SAUD

(b. 1880?–d. 1953)

The man who formed the modern nation of Saudi Arabia and who began petroleum exploration on the Arabian peninsula, Ibn Saud was a descendant of a dynasty that had ruled most of Arabia during the century prior to his birth. He was born about 1880 in the Saudi capital of Riyadh, and during his early years his family was driven from power by a rival dynasty, the Rashids. He grew up in poverty-stricken exile in Kuwait.

In 1901, at age 21, Ibn Saud began a nearly 30-year struggle to conquer and consolidate a kingdom. A daring raid into Riyadh in January 1902 succeeded in rousing the former supporters of his dynasty, and within two years he had won over much of central Arabia. Turkish forces summoned by the Rashids opposed him until 1912 with little success and then withdrew for lack of supply bases.

Ibn Saud, himself a devout Muslim, supported Wahhabism, an extremist Muslim puritan revival. To further aid his cause, he founded a militantly religious brotherhood known as the Ikhwan to combat Arab rivals and bring more tribesmen under his control. By 1922 he had totally extinguished the rule of the House of Rashid. In 1924 he seized the territory of the Hejaz, including the city of Mecca, from Sharif Husayn. In the late 1920s the Ikhwan turned against him when he forbade further raiding on their part. He defeated them at the Battle of Sibilla in March 1929, and three years later all of his domains were united into the nation of Saudi Arabia.

Ibn Saud's 20 years as absolute monarch were, in many ways, less fortunate than his time of struggle. In 1933 he signed his first oil exploration lease. Oil was discovered five years later, but work on the wells halted during World War II, leaving the country and government in poverty.

Once the oil money began coming in, the king was forced to watch the gradual encroachment of Western customs and irresponsible financial speculation. His puritan Muslim faith was offended by the great increase in corruption in government and society and by changing morals among his people. He spent his last years frustrated, unhappy, and plagued by ill health. He died on Nov. 9, 1953, at at-Ta'if and was succeeded by his son Saud.

THOMAS JEFFERSON

(b. 1743–d. 1826)

The author of the Declaration of Independence in 1776, Thomas Jefferson was later the third president of the United States, serving from 1801 to 1809. During his presidency the territory of the United States doubled with the Louisiana Purchase.

Thomas Jefferson was born on April 13 (April 2 according to the calendar used then), 1743, in Shadwell, Virginia. Jefferson entered the political arena in 1769 as a Virginia state legislator. From 1775 to 1801 he held several notable public positions including Continental Congress delegate, governor of Virginia, U.S. secretary of state, and vice president of the United States. As an activist for states' rights, Jefferson founded the Republican Party (later the Democratic-Republican Party). A Founding Father of his country, Jefferson inspired a sense of nationalistic pride for the United States based on liberty and human rights.

On January 1, 1772, Jefferson married Martha Wayles Skelton, a widow whose estate more than doubled Jefferson's landholdings when the couple combined their properties. Thomas and Martha Jefferson had six children, but only two girls survived childhood.

In 1769 Jefferson was elected to the House of Burgesses, Virginia's representative assembly, in Williamsburg. He emphasized that Great

Britain had no legal authority to govern and delegate authority in the colonies. In that same year the Virginia legislature appointed Jefferson as a delegate to the Second Continental Congress in Philadelphia. The Continental Congress recognized his idea for the colonies to secede from British rule as the best course of action.

On June 11, 1776, Jefferson was selected to a committee, which included John Adams and Benjamin Franklin, to outline a formal document justifying the reasons for declaring independence from Great Britain. The committee members admired Jefferson's talent for influential writing and chose him to prepare the first draft.

Portrait of Thomas Jefferson by artist Charles Wilson Peale. Courtesy Independence National Historical Park

The Continental Congress adopted the Declaration of Independence on July 4, 1776, which officially announced the separation of the 13 colonies from Great Britain. Jefferson and other delegates signed it, but he was not credited as the principal author until 1790. Between 1776 and 1777 the Continental Congress wrote the Articles of Confederation, which was ratified in 1781 as the first constitution of the United States.

Jefferson served as governor of Virginia before returning to national politics. With the assistance of his colleague, James Madison, Jefferson drafted the Virginia constitution complete with a declaration of rights. The two delegates proposed statutory reforms in Virginia that eventually set a standard for the entire country. Jefferson wrote the Virginia

Statute for Religious Freedom in 1777, which provided for the complete separation of church and state. People of Virginia were allowed to follow their own religious beliefs without political discrimination.

In 1781 he retired from public life after his term as governor and returned to his home at Monticello. Martha Jefferson died in September 1782, leaving Thomas to raise their two daughters, Patsy and Polly. He was devastated from the loss of his beloved wife and vowed never to marry again.

He sought to abolish slavery in any newly acquired U.S. territories and to free all slaves in the United States born after 1800. His proposal was defeated by a narrow margin in the Continental Congress.

The Continental Congress sent Jefferson to Paris in 1784 to succeed Benjamin Franklin as U.S. ambassador to France. The most controversial segment of Jefferson's personal life was his alleged love affair with his mulatto slave, Sally Hemings.

In the 1760 and '70s he and his fellow Virginia planters, all of whom owned slaves, supported the end of the slave trade in the colonies. By the time he returned to the United States in 1789, however, Jefferson had backed away from a leadership role against slavery.

Jefferson returned to the United States in 1789 to serve as secretary of state under George Washington, the first president of the United States. Jefferson and his political ally, James Madison, created the Republican Party (later Democratic-Republican Party), which was the forerunner of the present-day Democratic Party. Jefferson and Madison's party favored more autonomy within the state governments.

Jefferson ran for president with the support of the Republican Party. He was defeated by his political nemesis, John Adams, in a closely contested race. In the fiercely contested presidential election of 1800, Jefferson squared off against Adams in another competitive campaign between the Republicans and the Federalists, and was inaugurated into office on March 4, 1801.

U.S. delegates signed a treaty with Napoleon I in May 1803 for the Louisiana Purchase, which was Jefferson's most celebrated achievement as president. In 1804, Jefferson coasted to an easy victory in the presidential election.

Jefferson returned to Monticello in March 1809 after James Madison was inaugurated as the fourth president of the United States. He died at his home at Monticello on July 4, 1826, the 50th anniversary of the Declaration of Independence.

The Jefferson Memorial in Washington, D.C., was completed on April 13, 1943. A sculpture of Jefferson's head, representing the country's political philosophy, is one of four U.S. presidents carved into Mount Rushmore in southwestern South Dakota.

MOHAMMED ALI JINNAH

(b. 1876–d. 1948)

The founder of Pakistan was Mohammed Ali Jinnah. Failing to get Hindus and Muslims to work together, he was the main force behind India's partition in 1947 when Pakistan emerged as a separate Islamic nation.

Jinnah was born in Karachi (now in Pakistan) on Dec. 25, 1876. After attending school in the province of Sind, he studied law in London, England, from 1892 to 1896. He practiced law for ten years before entering politics. Because of his conviction that Muslims and Hindus could work together for the independence of India, he remained aloof from the All-India Muslim League until 1913. He became the league's president when he felt assured of its intent to cooperate with the Indian National Congress, the Hindu political party.

The emergence of Mahatma Gandhi and a series of Hindu revivalist movements drove a wedge between the two religious factions in the 1920s and 1930s. Frustrated, Jinnah moved to London in 1930, and remained there until he was persuaded to return home to help his people in 1935. Relations between the Hindu majority and Muslim minority deteriorated rapidly in the late 1930s, and by March 1940 the Muslim League had passed a resolution calling for a separate Islamic state. In 1947 the British government and the Indian National Congress agreed, and when India became independent from Britain on Aug. 15, 1947,

Pakistan was born. Jinnah served as Pakistan's first head of state until his death on Sept. 11, 1948, in Karachi.

RADOVAN KARADŽIĆ

(b. 1945–)

P oliticians Radovan Karadžić, nicknamed the "butcher of Bosnia," became the president of a breakaway Bosnian Serb republic. After he was indicted for war crimes in 1995 and forced to resign, he continued to run the Serb-controlled part of Bosnia and Herzegovina from a mountain hideaway outside the Bosnian capital of Sarajevo until he was arrested in 2008.

An ethnic Serb, Karadžić was born in the mountain village of Šavnik, Yugoslavia (now in Montenegro) on June 19, 1945. He was raised on old stories of Serbian independence wars against Muslim Turks and more recent stories of the slaughter of Serbs by Germans and Croats during World War II. Like many other peasants, he moved to Sarajevo at the age of 15 to seek prosperity in the city.

Karadžić studied medicine with a specialty in psychology. He met and married Ljiljana Zelen, a medical school classmate from a wealthy and socially prominent family. He studied at Columbia University in New York City in 1974–75. Back in Sarajevo he gambled heavily.

His first position as a psychiatrist was at Kosevo Hospital in Sarajevo. He worked in the 1970s and '80s for state hospitals and the Sarajevo soccer (association football) team among others. For extra income he sold fraudulent diagnoses to help patients avoid military service or to qualify for early retirement. He spent 11 months in jail in the mid-1980s on suspicion of misusing house loans in a business enterprise.

Karadžić became involved in the ethnic politics that emerged in Yugoslavia in the 1980s, after the death of dictator Tito. Karadžić helped establish the Serbian Democratic Party of Bosnia and Herzegovina (SDS) in 1990 to push a nationalist agenda. He warned that Bosnian Muslims were preparing a holy war to make Bosnia and Herzegovina a fundamentalist Islamic state. With the approval of Serbian President Slobodan Milošević, Karadžić was elected SDS party president.

When Muslims and Croats voted in 1992 to make Bosnia and Herzegovina an independent republic, Karadžić announced that Serbs could not live in such a state. The Bosnian Serbs formed their own break-away republic with the ultimate goal of unification with Serbia. They elected Karadžić president. When civil war broke out in April 1992, Karadžić and his associates moved their headquarters out of Sarajevo to the mountain village of Pale, 12 miles (19 kilometers) to the east.

Karadžić represented the Bosnian Serbs at peace talks in 1992 and 1993. Each negotiated cease-fire broke down. On April 23, 1995, a United Nations war crimes tribunal indicted Karadžić for his role in the mass murder of Bosnian Muslims.

Under international pressure, Milošević made Karadžić resign as president in July 1996. Karadžić's successor, Biljana Plavsic, found that Karadžić had been enriching himself at the country's expense, but she was powerless to do anything about it. Karadžić still con-trolled the republic from behind the scenes in Pale. Theoretically a fugitive from justice, he was confident the Bosnian Serbs would not arrest him.

In 1997, however, under mounting pressure, Karadžić went into hid-ing. Over the ensuing years he was spotted in Serbia, eastern Bosnia, Russia, and Montenegro. Despite his status as an international war criminal, he managed to publish a novel and still enjoyed the support of some Serb nationalists. On July 21, 2008, Serbian authorities finally arrested him near Belgrade, and he was transferred to The Hague, Netherlands, to await trial. It was then revealed that Karadžić had dis-guised himself and used an alias, Dragan Dabic, in order to practice alternative medicine openly in Belgrade. Karadžić's trial at The Hague opened in the fall of 2009.

HAMID KARZAI

(b. 1957–)

Hamid Karzai was the son and grandson of tribal leaders in Afghani-stan. Karzai upheld his family's tradition of governmental service by becoming his country's first elected president in 2004.

Born Dec. 24, 1957, in Kandahār, Afghanistan, Karzai was the son of the chief of the Popalzai Pashtuns. Under the Soviet-imposed regime in the 1980s, the Karzai family left Afghanistan and settled in Pakistan. Karzai attended Himachal Pradesh University in India, earning a master's degree (1982) in political science. During the Afghan War, he worked with the mujahideen, Islamic guerrilla fighters who sought to overthrow the Soviet-backed government, and often traveled to the United States to seek support for the cause. When the Communist government of Mohammad Najibullah fell in April 1992, the mujahideen established a coalition government, with Karzai serving as deputy foreign minister. In 1994, however, he resigned, tired of the infighting within the government. The growing strife escalated until the mujahideen turned on one another, and in the ensuing turmoil, the Taliban, an ultraconservative political and religious faction, came to power.

Although initially supportive of the Taliban and the order that it introduced to the country, Karzai came to oppose the regime and again went into exile in Pakistan. In July 1999 his father was assassinated, an act that he blamed on the Taliban and leadership of the Popalzai passed to Karzai. Shortly after the September 11 attacks in 2001, the United States led a military campaign to topple the Taliban and to capture terrorists that were based in the country. Karzai returned to Afghanistan to rally support for the U.S.-led mission, and by mid-November the Taliban regime had collapsed. Various Afghan groups, aided by the international community, named Karzai chair of an interim administration; he was sworn into office in late December 2001. In June 2002 a Loya Jirga, a traditional Afghan assembly, chose Karzai as president of a transitional government.

In January 2004, a new constitution was approved that called for a directly elected president. Later that year Karzai won the presidential election and was sworn into office. As Karzai entered office, he enjoyed strong support from Western allies, but he faced enormous challenges. Continued violence and instability and an inability to effectively build up Afghani institutions and provide basic services took its toll on his popularity at home and abroad, as did allegations of government corruption. The country was also plagued by an increase in drug trafficking as well as by the resurgence of the Taliban.

Karzai's term as president was due to expire in May 2009, and at that time he was constitutionally obligated to step down. Because of logistical and security reasons, however, the approaching presidential election—in which Karzai would be a candidate—was postponed from May to August of that year. Karzai asserted that for reasons of security he should remain in office until the election took place. Critics were concerned that maintaining his position would give Karzai an undue electoral advantage, and they urged him to step down as mandated by the constitution and turn power over to an interim government. In March 2009 the Supreme Court ruled that Karzai could legally retain his position until the election in August.

The presidential election was held on Aug. 20, 2009, and was followed by weeks of political turmoil. In September a preliminary count awarded Karzai almost 55 percent of the vote, thus indicating that he had won an outright victory over his closest challenger, former foreign minister Abdullah Abdullah. With more than 2,000 complaints of fraud and intimidation, however, the United Nations–backed Electoral Complaints Commission (ECC) ordered an audit of suspect polling stations and began an investigation into fraud allegations. In mid-October the ECC ruled that the fraudulent activity was pervasive enough to invalidate votes from more than 200 polling stations. As a result, Karzai's proportion of the vote slipped to 49.7 percent, low enough to warrant a second round of elections. Although Karzai initially resisted the call for a runoff, on October 20 he conceded to a second round of polling between himself and Abdullah. Shortly thereafter, however, Abdullah withdrew from the race, a decision he cited as being in the country's best interest. The runoff election was canceled, and shortly thereafter Karzai was inaugurated as president for a second term.

RUHOLLAH KHOMEINI

(b. 1902–d. 1989)

In January 1979 a revolution overthrew Mohammad Reza Shah Pahlavi, the shah, or monarch, of Iran, one of the wealthiest and best-armed nations in the Middle East. The moving force behind the revolution was the Shi'ah sect of Islam, led by Ayatollah Ruhollah Khomeini. The goal of the revolution was to establish an Islamic state based on the teachings of the Koran, Islam's holy book.

Khomeini was born in Khomeyn, Iran, in 1902. His father, also an ayatollah, was the leader of the local Shi'ite sect. After his father was killed, Ruhollah was brought up by an older brother. His entire education was in Islamic schools. As an adult he published a number of books on Islamic law, philosophy, and ethics. He was eventually recognized as an ayatollah, a religious title of honor meaning "sign of God." In 1962 he made his home in Qom, one of Iran's leading Shi'ite centers.

Khomeini became a strong critic of the shah, opposing his land-reform policies and his goal of making Iran a wealthy and modern nation, patterned after Western societies. He was briefly imprisoned for his criticisms, and in November 1964 he was banished from Iran altogether.

He settled in An Najaf, Iraq, until 1978 when he was asked to leave because of the problems he was causing within the Muslim community and his antagonism to neighboring Iran. Khomeini then moved to France, where he continued his agitation for the overthrow of the shah. From Paris he received worldwide exposure through the press. He sent taped messages to Iran that were transmitted by shortwave radio from the nation's mosques. Mounting public opposition forced the shah to leave the country on Jan. 16, 1979. Khomeini arrived on February 1 to take over the government. In December a new constitution created an Islamic republic, with Khomeini named as Iran's political and religious leader for life.

Khomeini wielded considerable power as sweeping changes were made throughout the country. The revolution did not bring peace to Iran. The country was beset with civil strife, economic decline, an eight-year war with Iraq, and opposition from other nations. Khomeini died in Tehran on June 3, 1989, and millions of mourners attended his funeral. A power struggle ensued within the government regarding his successor.

KIM IL-SUNG

(b. 1912–d. 1994)

When a separate North Korean government was established in 1948, Kim Il-Sung of the dominant Korean Workers' (Communist) Party became its leader. The first premier of North Korea, he became president under a new constitution in 1972. He ruled North Korea as a dictator until his death in 1994.

Kim Song-Ju was born on April 15, 1912, near Pyongyang, Korea. He joined the Korean Communist Party in 1931. During the 1930s he led armed resistance to the Japanese occupation of Korea and took the name Kim Il-Sung from an earlier anti-Japanese guerrilla fighter. After leading a Korean force in the Soviet army during World War II, he returned in 1945 to establish a Communist government under Soviet auspices in what would become North Korea.

In 1950 Kim Il-Sung made an unsuccessful attempt to extend his rule to South Korea, thereby starting the Korean War. With Chinese aid, he then repelled a subsequent invasion of North Korea by U.S. troops and other forces of the United Nations. The war ended in a stalemate in 1953.

As head of state, Kim eliminated all political opposition and became his country's absolute ruler. The twin goals of his regime were industrialization and the reunification of the Korean peninsula under North Korean rule. North Korea's state-run economy grew rapidly in the 1950s and '60s but eventually faltered, with shortages of food occurring by the early '90s. In his foreign policy Kim allied North Korea with the Soviet Union and China and remained hostile to South Korea and the United States. His rule went unchallenged for 46 years largely because of a propaganda system that promoted a personality cult centered on Kim as Korea's "Great Leader."

In 1994 Kim's desire to start a nuclear weapons program led to urgent international efforts to avoid war and to negotiate reunification. He died on July 8, 1994, just weeks before the talks were to begin. He was succeeded by his son, Kim Jong Il. A revised constitution introduced in 1998 enshrined Kim Il-Sung as "eternal president of the republic."

KIM JONG-EUN

(b. 1983 –)

The death of North Korean leader Kim Jong Il in 2011 brought his youngest son, Kim Jong-Eun, to power. He represented the third generation of the Kim dynasty, which had ruled North Korea since its creation in 1948.

Kim Jong-Eun (also spelled Kim Jong Un) was born in North Korea in

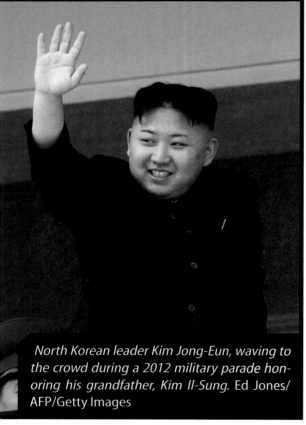

about 1983. He had lived most of his life out of the public eye, and little was known about him. Reportedly educated in Gümligen, Switzerland, at the International School of Berne, he went on to study at Kim Il-Sung National War College in Pyongyang from 2002 to 2007. As a young adult, Kim Jong-Eun began accompanying his father on military inspections. It was thought that he worked either for the Korean Workers' Party (KWP; the country's ruling party) or in the army's General Political Bureau; both organizations were involved in surveillance of government officials.

North Korean leader Kim Jong-Eun, waving to the crowd during a 2012 military parade honoring his grandfather, Kim Il-Sung. Ed Jones/AFP/Getty Images

Rumors began to circulate early in 2009 that he was

being groomed as his father's eventual successor. He was listed as a candidate for the legislature, the Supreme People's Assembly, in 2009. That April he was given a post on the powerful National Defense Commission (NDC); the chairmanship of the NDC, defined in the constitution as the country's highest office, was held by Kim Jong Il. By mid-2009 Kim Jong-Eun was being referred to within the country by the title "Brilliant Comrade," and in June it was reported that he had been named head of the State Security Department, the government agency responsible for political control and counterintelligence.

In September 2010 Kim Jong-Eun was given the high rank of four-star general, even though he was not known to have had any previous military experience. The timing of his appointment was considered significant, as it came shortly before the first general meeting of the KWP since the session in 1980 at which his father had been named Kim Il-Sung's successor. Over the next year his position as successor appeared to become more solidified. After the death of his father in December 2011, Kim Jong-Eun was declared the country's "supreme leader," an unofficial title that nonetheless signaled his position as the head of both the government and North Korea's military.

KIM JONG IL

(b. 1941–d. 2011)

From 1994 to 2011 Kim Jong Il ruled North Korea as one of the world's most repressive dictators. He succeeded his father, Kim Il-Sung, who had led the country since its founding in 1948. Kim took steps to reduce North Korea's long-standing isolationism but also engaged in provocative acts that raised the ire of South Korea and the world at large.

Kim Jong Il was born on February 16, 1941, in Siberia, Russia, then part of the Soviet Union. However, the official North Korean version of his life, differing from the biography documented elsewhere, says that he was born at a guerrilla base camp on Mount Paektu, the highest point on the Korean peninsula. It also claims that his birth was accompanied by such auspicious signs as the appearance of a double rainbow in the sky.

During the Korean War of 1950–53, Kim was placed in safety in northeastern China by his father, though the official biography does not mention the episode. After attending a pilots' training college in East Germany for two years, he graduated in 1963 from Kim Il-Sung University. He served in numerous routine posts in the Korean Workers' (Communist) Party (KWP) before becoming his father's secretary. In 1973 Kim was appointed to the powerful position of party secretary in charge of organization, propaganda, and agitation.

Kim was officially named his father's successor in 1980, was given command of the armed forces in 1990–91, and served in more high-ranking KWP posts. When Kim Il-Sung died in 1994, Kim Jong Il became North Korea's leader. He was named chairman of the KWP in 1997, and in 1998 he formally assumed the country's highest post. Since the position of president had been eliminated by the legislature, which reserved for Kim Il-Sung the title of "eternal president," the younger Kim was reelected chairman of the National Defense Commission, which became the country's highest office.

With his country facing a struggling economy and a famine, Kim made moves toward amending North Korea's policy of isolationism. Beginning in the late 1990s Kim sought to improve ties with a number of countries. In addition, he appeared to abide by the terms of a 1994 agreement (called the Agreed Framework) with the United States in which North Korea promised not to develop nuclear weapons. In 2000 Kim met with South Korean leader Kim Dae-Jung. In what was the first summit between leaders of the two countries, an agreement was reached to take steps toward reunification.

At the same time, however, the Agreed Framework began falling apart amid suspicions that North Korea had resumed its nuclear program. Relations with the United States deteriorated greatly in 2002, after U.S. President George W. Bush characterized Kim's regime (along with Iran and Iraq) as part of an "axis of evil." In 2003 Kim announced that North Korea was planning to develop nuclear weapons. The country conducted underground tests of such weapons in 2006 and 2009.

Kim's nuclear program was one of several factors that inflamed tensions with South Korea. The 2007 election of Lee Myung-Bak as the South Korean president brought a further decline in North-South relations as Lee took a harder line with his North Korean counterpart. Tensions between North and South reached a crisis point several times—notably in 2010, with the sinking of a South Korean warship in March and a November military skirmish on the South Korean island of Yeongpyeong that killed four South Koreans.

In 2008 speculation began that Kim's health was failing. The following year Kim and the North Korean political establishment began a series of moves apparently toward designating Kim's youngest son, Kim Jong-Eun, as his successor. The younger Kim ascended to power on December 19, 2011, two days after the death of Kim Jong Il.

HELMUT KOHL

(b. 1930–)

A prime force in bringing about the reunification of Germany in 1990, Helmut Kohl served as West Germany's chancellor from 1982 to 1990. He then became the first head of the reunited country, serving from 1990 to 1998.

Helmut Michael Kohl was born on April 3, 1930, in Ludwigshafen, a Rhine River port in what became the state of Rhineland-Palatinate. His father, Hans Kohl, was a civil servant who founded the local Christian Democratic Union (CDU) organization after World War II. Although he was too young to serve in the war, he searched for victims in bombed buildings.

From 1950 to 1958 Kohl studied law, political science, and history at the University of Frankfurt and the University of Heidelberg, where in 1958 he received a Ph.D. in history. He was a leader of the CDU members in the Ludgwigshafen city council from 1960 to 1967. He was the youngest person ever to become a member of the Rhineland-Palatinate state legislature (1959–69), state minister-president (1969–76), federal chairman of the CDU (1973–98), and West German chancellor (1982–90).

Kohl ran for chancellor of the Federal Republic of Germany, losing to Helmut Schmidt of the Social Democratic Party of Germany (SPD) and becoming the opposition leader in the Bundestag, Germany's lower house of parliament. In 1982 the Free Democratic Party withdrew from the SPD governing coalition. The coalition it formed with the CDU and Christian Social Union set the stage for Kohl to win the chancellorship on a parliamentary vote.

Kohl led coalition governments after victories in 1983 and 1987. His popularity then waned but improved as he worked toward reunification. His negotiations with Mikhail Gorbachev in mid-1990 assured that the new Germany would be part of the North Atlantic Treaty Organization. On Oct. 1, 1990, he led a conference that merged the East German and West German CDUs and became chancellor after reunification on October 3. On December 2 he won an easy victory in the first general election of the new Federal Republic of Germany. Kohl was reelected in 1994, but his popularity declined thereafter. In 1998 his 16-year term as Germany's chancellor came to an end when his party was defeated in national elections by the Social Democratic Party.

After being implicated in a scandal involving the CDU's taking illegal campaign contributions, Kohl stepped down from his party offices in 2000. The government fined him for his involvement in the affair in 2001.

VLADIMIR ILICH LENIN

(b. 1870–d. 1924)

F ew individuals in modern history had as profound an effect on their times or evoked as much heated debate as the Russian revolutionary Vladimir Lenin.

Lenin's birth name was Vladimir Ilich Ulyanov. He was born on April 22, 1870, the third of five children of a well-to-do Russian family. Ilya Lenin, Vladimir's father, served as a high-level education bureaucrat in the czar's government.

The death of Ilya Ulyanov in 1886 was followed by the arrest and execution of Alexander Ulyanov by the czarist secret police in March 1887. By his own admission, the unexpected arrest and execution of his older brother had a profound influence on Vladimir Ulyanov.

Several months after the death of Alexander, Vladimir enrolled at the University of Kazan to study law. In December 1887 officials from the school expelled him for his role in a student demonstration. In 1897 he was arrested for spreading propaganda among workers in St. Petersburg and exiled to Siberia. While in Siberia, Ulyanov married Nadezhda Krupskaya, a fellow Marxist whom he had known from St. Petersburg. Ulyanov served his exile in a town near the Lena River, and it was from the name of this river that he took the pseudonym that would remain with him until the end of his days.

In 1900, Lenin and Krupskaya were released from exile. Eager to reestablish unity among the Russian Marxists, Lenin and his wife traveled to Geneva,

Russian leader Vladimir Lenin, addressing a crowd. Hulton Archive/Getty Images

Switzerland, where they sought out the foremost Russian Marxist revolutionary group. Lenin proposed that the Geneva expatriates publish a new journal, known as *Iskra* (The Spark), to serve as a mouthpiece for orthodox Marxist theories.

In 1903, the *Iskra* group, as well as the entire Russian Social Democratic Workers Party, split into two different ideological camps. Lenin claimed for his group the name Bolsheviks (Majorityites). The other group was headed by a leader called Martov, accepted the title of Mensheviks (Minorityites).

When World War I broke out in August 1914, Lenin was the only prominent Russian Socialist to take a radical stance on the war. He denounced it and called on the working peoples of all nations to instead use their weapons to overthrow their capitalist governments.

In February 1917 (March 1917 by the modern calendar), spontaneous revolution broke out in Petrograd (which had been renamed from St. Petersburg at the beginning of World War I), and Czar Nicholas II was forced to abdicate.

Lenin returned to Russia in disguise at the end of October. On the evening of Oct. 26 (November 6 according to the modern calendar), 1917, the Bolsheviks, meeting in secret, resolved to overtake the government and establish a new provisional government. By the morning of October 27, the city of Petrograd was in Bolshevik hands.

Following the pacification of Russia's major cities, Lenin declared the formation of the world's first Communist government. Opposition groups were banned and newspapers and journals of other political groups were shut down. Banks and industries throughout the country were placed under the control of the new government. The Bolshevik government outlawed the ownership of most private property.

Lenin set out to make good on his promise for peace. He immediately opened negotiations with Germany to end the war. In March 1918 the Bolshevik government, with its Russian and German opponents at its throat, hesitatingly signed the Brest-Litovsk peace agreement, ending the war with Germany.

The signing of the Brest-Litovsk treaty sparked civil war in Russia. Lenin instituted a series of drastic and radical measures, known as War Communism. In July 1918, the Bolshevik government issued the most notorious of its edicts when it ordered Red Army troops to carry out the murder of Nicholas II and his entire family.

Lenin called the violent tactics the "Red Terror," and he vowed to destroy enemies of the state, both real and perceived. Estimates of the human toll of the Red Terror range from roughly 13,000 to more than 140,000. The civil war exacted its toll on Russia and on Lenin. By the time of the final Bolshevik victory in 1921, the country lay in absolute ruin. Lenin, in an effort to begin the rebuilding of the economy, issued a decree ending the draconian laws of War Communism. In its place, Lenin instituted the New Economic Policy, which allowed for a modest resumption of capitalist relations.

Lenin suffered two strokes and a third in 1923 that severely impaired his ability to function. A final stroke on Jan. 21, 1924, ended his life.

During the Soviet era, Lenin was hailed as the greatest national hero of the country. His writings ranked with those of Marx. Lenin's tomb, in Red Square in Moscow, was a national shrine. In 1924 Petrograd was renamed Leningrad in his honor. The citizens of Leningrad in 1991 voted to restore the city's name to St. Petersburg.

ABRAHAM LINCOLN

(b. 1809–d. 1865)

The 16th president of the United States, Abraham Lincoln, ranks among the greatest of all American statesmen. Lincoln came to the presidency at a time of great crisis, with the country at the brink of a civil war that threatened to split the North from the South. Combining his roles as statesman and commander in chief, Lincoln led the federal armies to victory and held the Union together. Along the way he brought about the end of slavery in the United States.

Abraham Lincoln was born at Sinking Spring near Hodgenville on Feb. 12, 1809. His birthplace was a one-room log cabin. In 1834 Lincoln was elected to the Illinois General Assembly. He was reelected again in 1836, 1838, and in 1840.

Encouraged by friends in the legislature, Lincoln decided to become a lawyer. He received his law license

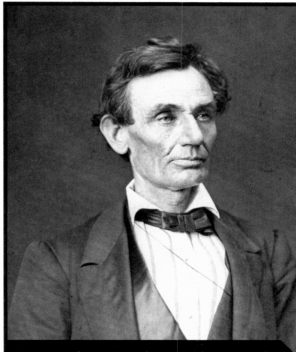

Portrait of U.S. President Abraham Lincoln.
Library of Congress Prints and Photographs Division

in 1836 and in April 1837 Lincoln left New Salem to make his home in Springfield. He soon made a reputation for himself as a lawyer, and became attracted to a society belle named Mary Todd whom he married on Nov. 4, 1842.

The threat of slavery being extended brought Lincoln back into the thick of politics in 1854. He did not suggest interfering with slavery in states where it was already lawful. The Kansas-Nebraska Act of 1854, however, enabled the people of each new territory to vote on whether the territory would be slave or free, thus threatening to extend slavery. Lincoln gave a series of speeches protesting the act.

In 1856 he helped to organize the Illinois branch of the new Republican Party, a political party formed by people who wanted to stop the spread of slavery. He became the leading Republican in Illinois. Lincoln received 110 votes for nomination as vice president. The Republicans lost the presidential election, but in 1858 Lincoln won the Republican nomination for senator from Illinois. He lost the election, but his speeches earned him a national reputation.

Realizing his countrywide fame, Lincoln's friends sought the Republican nomination for president for him in 1860. He now knew what he wanted—to be president of the United States in its time of crisis. He was determined to preserve the Union. At the Republican National Convention in Chicago, he was nominated on the third ballot.

On Nov. 6, 1860, Lincoln was elected 16th president of the United States. Alarm spread through the Southern states. They formed their own government, calling themselves the Confederate States of America. In his inaugural address, delivered on March 4, 1861, Lincoln assured the South that he would respect its rights, that there was no need for war. Nevertheless, less than six weeks later, on April 12, 1861, the Civil War began when Confederate forces fired on U.S. troops at Fort Sumter. The president shouldered the giant task of bringing the rebel states back into the national family and preserving the Union.

Lincoln was deeply devoted to the cause of personal freedom. Yet, as president, he was at first reluctant to adopt an abolitionist policy. He had been elected on a platform pledging no interference with slavery. Yet Lincoln knew that the slavery question must be settled if the United States, founded on the principles of liberty and equal rights for all, were to survive as a country. He realized that the Union must be preserved, as a free nation, if democratic government was to succeed in the world.

As antislavery sentiment rose, Lincoln worked out a plan to emancipate, or free, the slaves. On Sept. 22, 1862, Lincoln put forth his preliminary proclamation. It promised freedom for slaves in any Confederate state that did not return to the Union that year. When the South ignored him, he issued the final Emancipation Proclamation on Jan. 1, 1863. It was a landmark moment. It transformed the war from a struggle to preserve the Union into a crusade for human freedom.

Lincoln justified the Emancipation Proclamation as an exercise of the president's war powers. In 1865 Lincoln urged Congress to approve the 13th Amendment to the Constitution, which outlawed slavery in the United States.

In July 1863 the Union armies turned back the Confederate forces at Gettysburg, Pa. As an afterthought, Lincoln was invited "to make a few appropriate remarks." In a little less than three minutes he finished his inspiring Gettysburg Address.

Lincoln was reelected in 1864. To celebrate the end of the war, Lincoln took Mary and two guests to Ford's Theatre on the night of April 14, 1865. John Wilkes Booth, a young actor who was pro-slavery and a Confederate sympathizer crept into the presidential box and shot Lincoln in the head. Booth then leapt onto the stage, and, brandishing a dagger, he escaped.

Lincoln died without regaining consciousness. A funeral train carried the president's body back home to Springfield, Ill., where he lies buried in Oak Ridge Cemetery. The Lincoln Memorial in Washington, D.C., was dedicated to him in 1922.

LOUIS XIV

(b. 1638–d. 1715)

Louis XIV inherited power from his father. Styled the Grand Monarch, his court at Versailles became the model and the despair of other less rich and powerful princes, who accepted his theory of absolute monarchy (*L'état c'est moi*, "I am the state"). Until 1661 the government was largely in the hands of Italian Cardinal Mazarin. At the cardinal's death Louis declared that he would be his own prime minister. From then on he worked faithfully at his "trade of a king."

A passion for fame and the desire to increase French territory in Europe were Louis XIV leading motives. He neglected opportunities to gain an empire in America and India and involved France in wars that ruined it financially and paved the way for the outbreak of the French Revolution.

His first war, fought from 1667 to 1668, was an attempt to enforce flimsy claims to part of the Spanish Netherlands (Belgium). His second (1672–78) was directed against "their High Mightinesses," the States-General of Holland, who had blocked his objective in the first contest. The Dutch admiral De Ruyter twice defeated the fleets of the French and their English allies, and Louis XIV failed ingloriously in his attempt to conquer Holland. The third war (1689–97) also was directed chiefly against Holland, whose stadholder had by then become King William III of England. Louis's last and greatest effort was the War of the Spanish Succession (1701–13). In this conflict the English duke of Marlborough was the principal leader of the opposing European coalition.

The right to seat his grandson Philip V on the throne of Spain was small compensation for the thousands of lives and the millions in treasure that the French king wasted. Millions more were spent by Louis in building the palace at Versailles and in maintaining his court. There, etiquette became the "real constitution of France." It required seven persons, some of them the highest princes of the realm, to put the king's shirt on him at his getting up (*levée*) in the morning. A French historian said that he was "was a god in his temple, celebrating his own worship in the midst of his host of priests and faithful." This extravagance of the court meant a heavy burden of taxation for the common people, who were thereby reduced to a misery so great that they eventually rose up in rebellion and drove the Bourbons from the throne.

Louis XIV had the distinction of ruling longer than any other European king: it was 72 years from the time he ascended the throne, as a child of less than 5, until his death in 1715. The Grand Monarch, who had outlived both his son and his son's son, was succeeded by his 5-year-old great-grandson, Louis XV, the last son of the duke of Burgundy.

NELSON MANDELA

(b. 1918 –)

Nelson Mandela was a leader in the struggle against apartheid—South Africa's official system of segregation and discrimination against the country's non-white majority. He became a worldwide symbol of victory against that system when he was freed from his life sentence in prison.

Nelson Mandela was born into the royal family of the Tembu, a Xhosa-speaking people, on July 18, 1918, near Umtata, in the Transkei region of South Africa. He was originally named Rolihlahla Mandela; one of his school teachers gave him the English name Nelson. He studied at the University College of Fort Hare but was suspended in 1940 along with Oliver Tambo for taking part in a student protest. He earned a bachelor's degree from the University of South Africa in 1941 and began studying law. In 1952 he and Tambo opened the first black-owned law firm in South Africa.

In 1944 Mandela joined a black-liberation organization called the African National Congress (ANC) and helped found its influential Youth League. Mandela quickly rose to a position of leadership in the ANC, becoming a member of its National Executive Committee in 1949. His first jail sentence, which was suspended, was for helping lead the ANC's 1952 Defiance

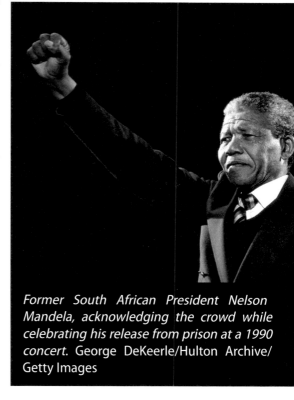

Former South African President Nelson Mandela, acknowledging the crowd while celebrating his release from prison at a 1990 concert. George DeKeerle/Hulton Archive/Getty Images

Campaign, in which thousands of volunteers peacefully violated the apartheid laws. Along with many other ANC leaders, Mandela was arrested and tried for treason in 1956. After a long trial, he was acquitted in 1961. Mandela divorced his first wife and married Nomzamo Winnie Madikizela (Winnie Mandela) in 1958 (they divorced in 1996).

The ANC's anti-apartheid protests had at first been wholly nonviolent. In 1960, however, after the police shot more than 200 unarmed black protesters at Sharpeville and the government banned the ANC, Mandela began to advocate acts of sabotage. He helped found a military wing of the ANC, called Umkhonto we Sizwe (Spear of the Nation), and became a fugitive.

In 1962 Mandela was caught and sentenced to five years in prison. A year later, while he was still serving that sentence, he was tried for sabotage, treason, and violent conspiracy, and in 1964 he was sentenced to life in prison. Mandela was kept in Robben Island Prison, off Cape Town, until 1982, when he was transferred to the maximum-security Pollsmoor Prison. Winnie Mandela spearheaded a campaign to free him, which gained vast support among both South Africa's black population and the international community that condemned apartheid. Mandela was set free on Feb. 11, 1990, by the administration of President F. W. de Klerk.

Once freed, Mandela continued with vigor the work of ending apartheid. He became the ANC's deputy president in March 1990 and its president in July 1991. In that office, he negotiated landmark agreements with de Klerk to bring about the peaceful transformation of South Africa into a majority-rule democracy. Mandela and de Klerk shared the 1993 Nobel Peace Prize for their achievements.

Along with millions of other black South Africans, Mandela voted for the first time in the election that brought him to power in April 1994. During his presidency, Mandela focused on improving the living standards of the country's black population, while advocating peaceful reconciliation with the white population. In 1995 he established the Truth and Reconciliation Commission (TRC) to investigate human rights violations committed during the apartheid era. He signed into law a new democratic constitution in 1996. The following year, Mandela resigned his post with the ANC. He retired from active politics in

1999, after his term as the country's president ended. Mandela married Graça Machel, the widow of former president of Mozambique Samora Machel, in 1998. His autobiography, *Long Walk to Freedom*, was published in 1994. In 2013, Mandela was hospitalized for several months with a lung infection, marking his 95th birthday while recuperating.

MAO ZEDONG

(b. 1893–d. 1976)

In China Mao Zedong is remembered and revered as the greatest of revolutionaries. His achievements as ruler, however, have been deservedly downgraded because he was among the worst of politicians. He knew well how to make a revolution, but once in power he could not put his love of revolution aside for the sake of governing.

Mao was born on Dec. 26, 1893, in Shaoshan, Hunan Province. During the Revolution of 1911–12 he served in the army for six months and graduated from the First Provincial Normal School in Changsha in 1918. He then went to Peking University, where he became embroiled in the revolutionary May Fourth Movement. This movement marked the decisive turn in Chinese revolutionary thought in favor of Marxist Communism as a solution to China's problems.

In 1921 Mao helped found the Chinese Communist Party. He was at that time a school principal in Hunan. Two years later, when the Communists forged an alliance with Sun Yat-sen's Nationalist Party (the Kuomintang), he left work to become a full-time revolutionary. It was at this time that Mao discovered the great potential of the peasant class for making revolution. This realization led him to the brilliant strategy he used to win control of China: gain control of the countryside and encircle the cities.

The Communists and the Nationalists coexisted in an uneasy relationship until the end of World War II. The Nationalist leader after 1925 was Chiang Kai-shek, who was determined to rule China. He never trusted the Communists, and at times he persecuted them. Mao's first wife was executed by the Nationalists in 1930.

The Chinese Soviet Republic was founded in November 1931 in Jiangxi Province. In 1934 Mao and his forces were driven out, and they went northward in what is known as the Long March. By 1935, however, the Communists and Nationalists forged a united front against the Japanese, which persisted despite rivalries till 1945. The revolution that then began ended in 1949 with the Communists victorious.

In addition to his problems with the Nationalists, Mao's dealings with the Soviet Union's Joseph Stalin were always uneasy. Stalin grew wary of a competing Communist power of China's size on the Soviet borders. Mao eventually came to regard the Soviets as revisionists and felt they were traitors to the cause of world revolution.

Mao's title as ruler of China was chairman of the People's Republic. For the first five years he rarely appeared in public and seemed to be only a ceremonial figure. He never achieved the total control in China that Stalin did in the Soviet Union. Many of his comrades were influential in directing policy, often in ways with which Mao disagreed. In 1955 he emerged from isolation determined to play the decisive role in economic policy and political restructuring.

Failing to gain the allegiance of the intellectuals, he turned to the masses with a program called the Great Leap Forward. While not a complete economic disaster, it had severe consequences. After it disrupted both city and countryside, he was forced to retreat from his policies in favor of his opponents. To counter opposition he launched the Great Proletarian Cultural Revolution, urged on by his radical wife, Jiang Qing. This vast upheaval wrecked the Communist Party bureaucracy, paralyzed education and research, and left the economy almost a shambles.

Only slowly did China begin to recover. By then Mao was old and ill. Other, more moderate hands guided policy. Zhou Enlai seemed to emerge as the nation's real leader when relations were reestablished with the United States.

Mao's personality cult remained strong until his death on Sept. 9, 1976. Shortly afterward, however, a power struggle was under way. Members of the party who had been purged by the Cultural Revolution returned to govern China. Chief among them was Deng Xiaoping.

ANGELA MERKEL

(b. 1954–)

Noted for her political skill, politician Angela Merkel became the first female chancellor of Germany in 2005. In parliamentary elections four years later, she was reelected to the post.

Merkel was born Angela Dorothea Kasner on July 17, 1954, in Hamburg, West Germany. She moved with her family to East Germany when she was just a child. After earning a doctorate in physics at the University of Leipzig in 1978, she settled in East Berlin, where she worked at the Academy of Sciences as a quantum chemist. After becoming involved in the democracy movement in the 1980s, she joined the conservative Christian Democratic Union (CDU). In 1990 Merkel was elected to the lower house of parliament. She subsequently served under Chancellor Helmut Kohl as minister of family affairs, senior citizens, women, and youth from 1991 to 1994 and as minister of environment, conservation, and reactor safety from 1994 to 1998.

In 1998 Gerhard Schröder and the Social Democratic Party of Germany (SPD) won the elections from Kohl and the CDU. A year later Kohl was involved in a scandal arising from the collection of illegal campaign contributions. Merkel decisively shifted her support from Kohl, enhancing her visibility and popularity with the German voters. In 2000 she was elected head of the CDU, becoming the first woman and the first non-Catholic to lead the party. She was also the first CDU leader to come from the party's liberal wing, much to the disapproval of the CDU's sister party in Bavaria, the ultraconservative Christian Social Union (CSU). As a consequence, Merkel had to contend not only with the lingering effects of the finance scandal but also with a divided party. For the 2002 general elections the party nominated Edmund Stoiber of the CSU, who later lost to Schröder.

Merkel received the party's nomination for the 2005 election. In campaign promises she vowed to reform the country's struggling economy and repair relations with the United States, which had become strained by Schröder's opposition to the Iraq War. The CDU and CSU won the general election but did not capture a majority with its preferred coalition partner, the Free Democratic Party (FDP). After weeks of negotiations, a deal was reached with the SPD that gave Merkel the chancellorship in a coalition government. She took office in November 2005, becoming the first East German to hold the position. In September 2009 Merkel was reelected chancellor, this time with the CDU-CSU and the FDP winning enough seats to form a coalition without the SPD. She was awarded the U.S. Presidential Medal of Freedom in 2011.

SLOBODAN MILOŠEVIĆ

(b. 1941 – d. 2006)

While other Communist governments crumbled in the late 1980s, former Communist bureaucrat Slobodan Milošević rose to become the head of state of Serbia (1989–97) and then Yugoslavia (1997–2000). He used his control of the media, government appointments, police, and the military to rouse ethnic hatred and to build a Serbian nationalist mass movement. In 1999 Serbia launched a major offensive against an ethnic Albanian liberation group in the Serbian province of Kosovo. Milošević was later indicted for war crimes and tried by the International Court of Justice.

Milošević was born on Aug. 29, 1941, in Požarevac, Serbia, Yugoslavia. In high school he met Mirjana Marković, the daughter of a leading Serbian Communist family. They later married, and she became his political adviser.

Milošević completed his law degree at the University of Belgrade in 1964. An older law student, Ivan Stambolić, became his friend and mentor. As a loyal Communist, Milošević benefited from Marshal Tito's ouster of reformers from government-controlled positions in the 1970s. He was appointed manager of an energy plant and then president of a large Belgrade bank. His career continued to prosper after Tito died in 1980.

In 1984 Stambolić, who recently had been made Serbian Communist Party leader, appointed Milošević head of the Belgrade party committee. Belgrade was a center for liberal reformers and Serbian nationalists, but Milošević firmly suppressed the dissidents. He censored publications and promoted Marxism in the schools. In January 1986 Stambolić became president of Serbia, and Milošević replaced him as Serbian party chief.

Long-standing tensions in the autonomous province of Kosovo flared between the Serb minority and the ethnic Albanian majority in 1987. In response, Milošević adopted an aggressively pro-Serb stance, which brought him great popularity among the Serbs. He also used the issue to help turn the party against Stambolić. At a nationally televised party meeting, leading Communists severely criticized Stambolić's regime for its supposed failure to defend Serbian interests in Kosovo. Two months later Stambolić resigned.

Having orchestrated his former friend's downfall, Milošević ran Serbian politics from behind the scenes and built a base of support in the army. One of his first actions was to revoke the autonomous status of the provinces of Kosovo and Vojvodina. In May 1989 the parliament elected him president of Serbia. In July 1990, seeing Communism on the wane, he renamed his party the Socialist Party of Serbia. That December, Serbia held its first contested elections. Favored by the government-controlled media, Milošević won. Demonstrations against him broke out in March 1991.

By that time other Yugoslav republics were moving toward independence. Slovenia, Croatia, and Macedonia each declared their independence from Yugoslavia in 1991, as did Bosnia and Herzegovina in 1992. Serbia and Montenegro formed a new Yugoslav federation. Many Serbians worried about a backlash against the Serb minorities in Croatia and Bosnia. Milošević encouraged the Yugoslav army to attack Croatia and the Bosnian Serbs to seize land by force. In the civil wars that followed, he armed the Serbs in Croatia and Bosnia and roused ethnic hatred at home. Tens of thousands died in the wars. The Serbian campaign of "ethnic cleansing" sought to expel or eliminate the non-Serb majority in Croatia and Bosnia using mass executions, forced marches, torture, starvation, and systematic rape. In response, the United Nations imposed trade sanctions on Serbia, and the country's economy suffered. Milošević, however, easily won reelection as Serbian president in December 1992. In order to lift the sanctions, Milošević agreed to a peace settlement in 1995.

The war, lack of economic reform, and the Milošević family's accumulation of money and power alienated many of his supporters. After Milošević annulled opposition victories in local elections in November 1996, tens of thousands of protesters marched in the streets of Belgrade daily for months. He eventually recognized the results of the election, but his actions continued to provoke controversy.

Constitutionally unable to serve another term as president of Serbia, Milošević had the parliament name him president of Yugoslavia in July 1997. In 1998, in an attempt to crack down on rebels known as the Kosovo Liberation Army (KLA), Milošević began a campaign of terror against the Kosovo Albanians, who accounted for about 90 percent of the province's population. He ordered a major attack on the province the following year. The North Atlantic Treaty Organization (NATO) began an air bombardment against Yugoslavia in March to try to end the Serb aggression. The bombing galvanized support for Milošević, however, who then began a campaign of ethnic cleansing in Kosovo that drove out hundreds of thousands of Albanians. In May of that year the United Nations War Crimes Tribunal indicted Milošević and several associates on four counts of war crimes allegedly committed in Kosovo. After Yugoslavia had endured 11 weeks of bombing, the Milošević government agreed to terms of a peace settlement with NATO in June 1999.

In 2001 the government of Yugoslavia arrested him and turned him over to the International Court of Justice on charges that he committed genocide, crimes against humanity, and other war crimes during the conflicts in Croatia, Bosnia and Herzegovina, and Kosovo. His trial began in 2002 in The Hague. Delayed repeatedly by Milošević's bouts of illness, the trial was still under way when the former Serbian leader was found dead in his detention cell on March 11, 2006.

MOHAMMED MORSI

(b. 1951–)

Egyptian engineer and politician Mohammed Morsi was elected president of Egypt in 2012. He was the country's first democratically elected president.

Morsi was born on August 20, 1951, in Egypt's Sharqiyyah Governorate, on the eastern side of the Nile River delta. After studying at Cairo University, he continued his education in the United States, earning a Ph.D. in engineering from the University of Southern California in 1982. He later taught engineering at California State University, Northridge, and also worked for the National Aeronautics and Space Administration.

In 1985 Morsi returned to Egypt and became a professor of engineering at Zagazig University, a position that he held until 2010. He also became active in politics as a member of the Muslim Brotherhood. In 2000 he was elected to the People's Assembly; because the Muslim Brotherhood, an Islamist organization, was formally banned in Egypt, he held the seat as an independent. During this time he called on the government to lift repressive measures, including the emergency law, which granted the police unlimited powers of arrest and detention, and laws limiting the formation of political parties. He also established himself as a social conservative, urging tighter restrictions on entertainment that he considered indecent.

Morsi lost his seat in the People's Assembly in 2005, when the administration of Pres. Hosni Mubarak used electoral fraud to reverse the gains made by the Muslim Brotherhood in 2000. In 2006 Morsi was arrested and imprisoned for seven months after participating in protests calling for the establishment of an independent judiciary in Egypt. He was also arrested in early 2011 during the Arab Spring mass protests that forced Mubarak to step down as president.

Mubarak's ouster cleared the way for the Muslim Brotherhood to participate openly in Egyptian politics, and to that end the group formed the Freedom and Justice Party. In April 2012 the party selected Morsi to be its candidate in Egypt's presidential election. The next month Morsi received the most votes in the first round of balloting, advancing to a runoff with the second-place finisher, Ahmed Shafiq, a former military officer who had served as Mubarak's last prime minister. The runoff was held on June 16–17, and Morsi again came out on top, capturing 51.7 percent of the vote to Shafiq's 48.3 percent. Morsi was officially recognized as the winner of the election on June 24, 2012.

HOSNI MUBARAK

(b. 1928 –)

Muhammad Hosni Said Mubarak was born in Minufiya, a governate of Egypt, on May 4, 1928. In April 1975 Anwar Sadat named Mubarak vice president—a role in which he controlled Egyptian intelligence services and was active in the planning of Middle East and Arab policy. He became the chief mediator in the dispute between Morocco, Mauritania, and Algeria over the future of the Western Sahara.

Mubarak was the chosen successor of Sadat, who was killed by Muslim fundamentalists on October 6, 1981, the anniversary of the start of the 1973 Egyptian-Israeli war. In the April 1987 elections his National Democratic Party retained overwhelming control of the Egyptian legislature in spite of continued Muslim opposition to the government policy on Israel. After receiving 97 percent of the popular vote in an October referendum, he began his second term as president.

Under Mubarak diplomatic relations were resumed with other Arab states and Egypt regained status. In 1989 it was readmitted into the Arab League. Next Mubarak was elected chairman of the Organization of African Unity. After the Iraqi invasion of Kuwait in 1990, he deployed Egyptian troops as part of the multinational force in defense of Saudi Arabia. His tough stance won international admiration at the time, and his party won a sweeping legislative victory in November.

Reelected president in 1993, Mubarak faced a rise in guerrilla violence and growing unrest among opposition parties. He was reelected to a fourth term as president in 1999. In 2005 Mubarak easily won Egypt's first multicandidate presidential election, which was marred by low voter turnout and allegations of irregularities.

In January 2011 thousands of protesters—angered by repression, corruption, and poverty in Egypt—took to the streets, calling for Mubarak to step down as president. On January 29 Mubarak appointed a vice president for the first time in his presidency, choosing Omar Suleiman, the director of the Egyptian General Intelligence Service. On February 11, 2011, amid continuing protests by the Egyptian citizenry, Mubarak resigned as president, turning over power to the military.

Following Mubarak's departure, the Egyptian government began to investigate allegations of corruption and abuse of power within the Mubarak regime, questioning and arresting several former officials and business leaders with close ties to Mubarak. On April 10 the public prosecutor announced that Mubarak and his sons would be questioned by investigators. Following the announcement, Mubarak made his first public statements since stepping down as president, denying the accusations of corruption. On April 12, while waiting to be questioned, Mubarak was hospitalized after reportedly suffering a heart attack.

In May the public prosecutor announced that Mubarak would stand trial for ordering the killing of protesters as well as for corruption and abuse of power. In June 2012 an Egyptian court found Mubarak guilty of complicity in the deaths of demonstrators, and he was sentenced to life in prison.

ROBERT MUGABE

(b. 1924 –)

After Zimbabwe gained its independence, Robert Mugabe served as the country's first prime minister. He established one-party rule, assuming the office of executive president in 1987.

Robert Gabriel Mugabe was born on Feb. 21, 1924, in Kutama, then in the British colony of Southern Rhodesia. He attended the University of South Africa and the University of Fort Hare in South Africa. He taught in Southern Rhodesia until the late 1950s, when he moved to Ghana. There he was impressed by the radical politics of President Kwame Nkrumah. Mugabe returned to Southern Rhodesia in 1960 and worked with Joshua Nkomo in their country's nationalist movement. He broke with Nkomo's Zimbabwe African People's Union (ZAPU) in 1963, however, to help form the Zimbabwe African National Union (ZANU). His group advocated deposing by force Rhodesia's white supremacist government. In 1964 he was arrested for speaking against the government. While in prison he acquired six university degrees and also led a coup.

Mugabe was released in 1975 and, with Nkomo, helped organize guerrillas in the Patriotic Front (PF) to oppose Rhodesia's white-ruled government. In 1979 whites agreed to a new constitution allowing black rule, and the country, renamed Zimbabwe, achieved independence in 1980. As prime minister, Mugabe formulated a Marxist-socialist government. In 1987 ZAPU merged with Mugabe's party, which had been renamed ZANU-PF. Mugabe served as executive president of the one-party state and remained in this post after multiparty elections in 1990. The Central Committee of ZANU-PF deleted all references to Marxism-Leninism from the constitution in 1991.

Mugabe was reelected in 1996 and 2002. In 2008, amid a collapsing economy, he was forced into a runoff election. However, his opponent, Morgan Tsvangirai, claiming that fair elections were impossible, boycotted the runoff. Mugabe's uncontested victory prompted international condemnation as well as calls for a power-sharing government to be formed. As part of an agreement signed in September 2008, Mugabe remained president but ceded some power to Tsvangirai, who became prime minister in early 2009.

BENITO MUSSOLINI

(b. 1883–d. 1945)

Benito Mussolini was many things during his turbulent life—teacher, laborer, soldier, politician, and revolutionary. Conflict, ambition, and the desire for power brought him to the day in late October 1922 when he founded Fascism and became dictator of Italy. The same forces ultimately led to his violent death at the hands of his countrymen.

Mussolini was born in Dovia di Predappio, Italy, on July 29, 1883. He was named Benito for the Mexican revolutionary Juárez. A restless, disobedient child, he grew up a bully. He became a Socialist in his teens and worked, often as a schoolmaster, to spread the party doctrine.

World War I changed Mussolini. Once a reformer, he became a worshiper of power. Unlike most of the Socialists, he advocated Italy's entry into the war on the Allied side. Expelled from the Socialist party, he founded his own newspaper, *Il Popolo d'Italia* (The People of Italy), and called Italians to arms. In 1916 he enlisted. After being promoted to sergeant, he was wounded. In 1917 he returned to his newspaper.

During the chaos that gripped Italy after the war, Mussolini's influence grew swiftly. Into an army of supporters who wore black shirts (the symbolic uniform of anarchists) he recruited discontented Socialists, veterans, the unemployed—all the dissidents who believed that only a ruthless dictator could revitalize Italy. By 1922 crowds of peasants were spellbound by his magnetism and oratory and his backers were powerful enough to force King Victor Emmanuel III to bow before a Fascist march on Rome to seize the government. The king named Mussolini prime minister, Italy's youngest ever. He then became dictator and was called Il Duce (The Leader).

As dictator, Mussolini had the power to make all decisions. He built roads, harnessed rivers, increased production, and ran the trains on time. He tried to colonize Eritrea and Libya on a grand scale. In defiance of the League of Nations he invaded Ethiopia in 1935 and seized Albania in 1939. He boasted that he was regaining the glory and prestige of ancient Rome.

Mussolini's apparent triumphs encouraged Adolf Hitler to organize Germany on the Fascist pattern. They created a Rome-Berlin Axis of totalitarianism, but Mussolini became Hitler's pawn. Meanwhile his harsh rule had made enemies at home, and his international arrogance had helped pave the way to World War II. His army proved ineffectual, and German troops occupied Italy. After the Allies invaded Sicily in 1943, Mussolini was forced to resign. Rescued from prison by German troops, he set up a puppet rule for northern Italy, which was still under German control. In disguise he tried to escape from the Allied advance, but he and his mistress, Clara Petacci, were shot near Como by Italian partisans on April 28, 1945. Their bodies were exhibited to jeering crowds in the streets of Milan.

NAPOLEON I

(b. 1769–d. 1821)

To the troops he commanded in battle Napoleon was known fondly as the "Little Corporal." Napoleon I, emperor of the French and for 16 years master of most of Europe, was regarded as one of the greatest military geniuses of all time.

Napoleon Bonaparte was born in Ajaccio, on the island of Corsica, on Aug. 15, 1769. When he was nine years old, he was sent by his father to a French government military school. In 1784–85 he attended the École Militaire in Paris. There he received training as an artilleryman and as an officer. When his course was completed he joined the French army as a second lieutenant of artillery.

The French Revolution was a decisive event in Napoleon's life, for it gave him his opportunity to get ahead. In October 1795 a great opportunity came his way. The people of Paris were tired of war and privations. They rose against the Convention, the French legislative body. Napoleon was appointed to put down the revolt. Coolly, he took complete control. The Convention was saved, and a new government, the Directory, was formed.

Napoleon was made commander of the army in Italy, which was then fighting the Austrians and their allies. The Italian campaign showed Napoleon's military genius. In 1796 he defeated the Sardinian troops five times in 11 days, threatened Turin, their capital, and forced the king of Sardinia to sue for peace.

He besieged a part of the Austrian forces in Mantua and had advanced to within 80 miles of Vienna when the enemy surrendered. Napoleon had been victorious in 14 pitched battles and 70 combats. Napoleon's return from Italy to Paris was a triumph. No other general of the Revolution had received such a welcome. He now began to think of political as well as military power.

Napoleon joined in a plot which, in November 1799, overthrew the Directory. In its place was set up a government called the Consulate, with Napoleon as the first of the three consuls. He was now the people's hero. Within three years he was made first consul for life. He now called himself Napoleon I instead of General Bonaparte. He held complete military and political power.

The peace meantime was an uneasy one. In May 1803 war broke out again between France and England. Only England stood in the way of his complete mastery of Western Europe. In 1805 he had planned to invade Great Britain. The favorable moment never came. England's navy, under Adm. Horatio Nelson, had destroyed the French fleet at Trafalgar, Oct. 21, 1805.

In 1804 he had secured a popular vote changing the French government from a consulate to an empire. Now he needed an heir—one of undeniably royal blood. In 1809 he divorced his wife Josephine after their marriage produced no heir. In 1810 he took as his bride Marie Louise, the 18-year-old daughter of the emperor of Austria. Within a year she had given him a son whom he named the king of Rome.

Artist's rendering of Napoleon crossing the Alps. Leemage/Hulton Fine Art Collection/Getty Images

Napoleon decided to invade Russia. It was not the best time to do so. With a Grand Army drawn from 20 nations he plunged boldly into the vastnesses of Russia. The campaign was to prove a disaster. Russian military tactics included a scorched-earth policy. Russian winters were incredibly severe. These were a combination of conditions Napoleon had never before experienced. Always the Russians retreated before him, drawing him deeper and deeper into their country.

In September 1812, Napoleon reached Moscow. He found the city in flames. Since it was impossible to winter in the ruined city, Napoleon began his retreat on October 19 across the snow-covered plains. The retreat from Moscow was one of the great disasters of military history. Of the nearly 500,000 men who had set out in June, fewer than 20,000 ragged, freezing, and starving men staggered back across the Russian frontier in December.

Now his enemies saw their chance. With the collapse of those once mighty armies, the nations seized the opportunity to overthrow their conqueror. England, Austria, and Prussia joined Russia in the War of

Liberation. In the three-day Battle of Leipzig—called the Battle of the Nations—the French were outnumbered, outgeneraled, and outfought.

On March 30, 1814, the allies captured Paris itself and Napoleon was forced to abdicate on April 6, 1814. He was sent into exile on the tiny island of Elba in Italy. In March 1815 he escaped and landed in France. He began a triumphal march on Paris, picking up support along the way.

For a brief time, known as the Hundred Days, Napoleon enjoyed a return to his former glory. It came to an end with the Battle of Waterloo, which was fought on June 18, 1815. Napoleon suffered his final defeat by a combined English and Prussian force.

His dream of a world empire came to a close on the tiny island of St. Helena, to which he was exiled on July 15, 1815. The island is located in the South Atlantic Ocean well off the coast of Africa. Napoleon died there, alone and deserted by his friends and family, on May 5, 1821.

GAMAL ABDEL NASSER

(b. 1918–d. 1970)

At the age of 16 Gamal Abdel Nasser led a student political demonstration in Cairo, Egypt. The students were protesting against British influence on Egypt's business enterprises and government. Thus began a turbulent career that ended only with Nasser's death at the age of 52. Although he ultimately failed to realize his dream of uniting the Arab world, he did succeed in gaining the widespread support of the Arab people throughout the Middle East.

Gamal Abdel Nasser was born on Jan. 15, 1918, in Alexandria, Egypt. He graduated from the Royal Military Academy of Egypt in 1938. After serving as a lieutenant in the Egyptian army, he was appointed an instructor at the Army Staff College in 1942. While at the college Nasser organized a secret society called the Free Officers Movement. During the Palestine campaign of 1948, in which he led Egyptian forces against Israel, Nasser laid plans for the society to seize the Egyptian government from King Farouk I.

On July 23, 1952, Nasser led his officers' group in the coup d'état that drove King Farouk I from his throne. Major General Mohammed

Naguib was chosen head of the government. Nasser was appointed to the offices of deputy premier and minister of the interior.

In 1954 Nasser forced Naguib out of office and assumed the premiership. He confiscated land from wealthy landlords for distribution among poor farmers. Under a new constitution that he proclaimed in 1956, Nasser was elected president of Egypt. Counting on aid from the United States and Great Britain, he hoped to start work on the Aswan High Dam, a hydroelectric and flood-control project on the Nile River, but the assistance did not materialize. Seeking an alternative source of funds, he nationalized the Suez Canal. Political crises that arose from that action included an Anglo-French invasion of the Canal Zone and the defeat of Egypt's armies by Israel.

In February 1958 Nasser was elected president of the United Arab Republic (UAR), formed by the union of Egypt and Syria. In 1961, however, Syria withdrew from the UAR. In 1962, when a revolt against the monarchy broke out in Yemen, Nasser sent troops to aid the insurgents. In an uncontested election in 1965 he was reelected president.

In 1967, after months of Arab-Israeli contention, Nasser closed the Gulf of Aqaba to Israeli shipping and massed UAR troops on the Israeli border. Following Egypt's defeat in the ensuing war, Nasser took responsibility for the disaster and resigned from public office. Acclaimed by the public and the National Assembly, he agreed to remain as president and assumed the premiership and the leadership of the UAR's only political party, the Arab Socialist Union. Soviet and Arab aid enabled Nasser to avert economic ruin. In 1968 his policies won overwhelming approval in a national plebiscite. That same year the Aswan High Dam, completed with the assistance of the Soviet Union, began operational. On Sept. 28, 1970, Nasser died at his villa near Cairo.

JAWAHARLAL NEHRU

(b. 1889–d. 1964)

For more than 20 years Jawaharlal Nehru worked with Mahatma Gandhi to free India from British rule. The two great leaders achieved their goal in 1947, when India became an independent country within the British Commonwealth. Nehru became the first prime minister of the new India.

Nehru was born in Allahabad, India, on Nov. 14, 1889. His ancestors were Kashmiri who had migrated from their native home in the early 1800s. His father, Motilal Nehru, was a leader of the Indian independence movement. When Jawaharlal was 16 he went to England to study at Harrow and later Cambridge. He returned to India in 1912 and became a lawyer in Allahabad.

Nehru met Gandhi in 1916 at the annual convention of the Indian National Congress Party, and he later became absorbed in Gandhi's campaign for Indian independence. In 1929 Nehru became the Congress Party's leader. Between 1921 and 1945 he was jailed nine times for his political activity. Between prison terms he traveled throughout India, winning support for Gandhi's program of nonviolent resistance to British rule. He was called Pandit, which means "wise man."

Nehru was equally at home in the cultures of India and the West. From Western economic and political thought he drew what he believed was best for India. He disliked Gandhi's idealization of the simple life. He aimed to make India a democratic socialist state, tolerant of all religions. In foreign policy, he tried to follow a path of nonalignment during the Cold War, not siding with either the United States or the Soviet Union, or their allies. Nehru retained office of prime minister in the 1952, 1957, and 1962 elections. He died in New Delhi on May 27, 1964.

Nehru's wife, Kamala, whom he had married in 1916, died in 1936. Their daughter, Indira, was the first lady of India during his years as prime minister. This led to her own political career; not long after he died she became prime minister of India, under her married name, Indira Gandhi. Her son, Rajiv Gandhi, also later served as prime minister.

Nehru's writings include an autobiography, collections of speeches and essays, and several historical works, including *Glimpses of World History* (1934–35) and *The Discovery of India* (1946). He wrote many of his works while in prison.

RICHARD M. NIXON

(b. 1913–d. 1994)

R ichard M. Nixon established cordial relations with Soviet Russia, was the first U.S. president to visit China, and oversaw ground-troop withdrawal near the end of the American involvement in the Vietnam War. Yet the event for which his presidency is best remembered was the Watergate scandal. Nixon was the first president of the United States to resign from office. Before his mid-term retirement in 1974, he had been only the second president to face impeachment.

Richard Milhous Nixon was born in Yorba Linda, a farming village in Orange County, Calif., on Jan. 9, 1913. At 17 Nixon entered Whittier College. He then won a scholarship to Duke University, in Durham, N.C. After graduating Nixon was admitted to the California bar and joined the firm of Wingert and Bewley in Whittier. A short time later it became Bewley, Knoop, and Nixon. In a Whittier theater group Nixon met "Pat" Ryan. On June 21, 1940, two years after their first meeting, they were married.

A few weeks after the United States entered World War II Nixon went to Washington. In

President Richard Nixon (front center, facing camera), meeting with Chinese leaders in 1972. Sovfoto/ Universal Images Group/Getty Images

September 1942 he was commissioned a lieutenant, junior grade in the navy and rose to the rank of lieutenant commander.

After the war Nixon returned to the United States, where he learnt that a Republican citizen's committee in Whittier was considering Nixon as a candidate for Congress in the 12th Congressional District. On Nov. 5, 1946, Richard Nixon won his first political election.

Nixon decided to run for the Senate. Nixon won the election, held on Nov. 7, 1950, and at 38 he became the youngest member of the Senate. His Senate career was uneventful, and he was able to concentrate all his efforts on the upcoming 1952 presidential election.

Nixon did his work well. He hammered hard at three main issues— the war in Korea, Communism in government, and the high cost of the Democratic Party's programs. At their 1952 national convention the Republicans chose him as Eisenhower's running mate.

The Republicans won the election by a landslide. Eisenhower groomed his vice president for active duty. Nixon regularly attended Cabinet meetings and meetings of the National Security Council. In the absence of the president he presided over these sessions.

In 1960 the Republican Party chose its seasoned vice president to run for the nation's highest office. Richard Nixon lost the presidential race by the narrow margin of about 100,000 votes. He had lost an election for the first time, and he seemed to be out of the political picture.

In 1964 Nixon made no move toward the presidency. He supported Barry M. Goldwater, the conservative Republican candidate and campaigned vigorously on Goldwater's behalf. In 1966 he traveled 30,000 miles and visited 35 states in behalf of 87 Congressional candidates. Between 1964 and 1967 he helped raise 5 to 6 million dollars for Republican campaign expenses. By the time the 1968 presidential campaign got under way Republicans all over the country owed Nixon support.

In the 1968 primary elections Nixon began to cast off the "loser" image. He won the Republican presidential nomination easily. On Nov. 5, 1968, Nixon's long and loyal support of his party was repaid, and he was elected the 37th president of the United States. In his inaugural address Nixon emphasized his determination to seek peace abroad, especially in Vietnam, and to bring about a reconciliation of the differences that divided the United States.

Upon becoming president, Nixon turned his attention primarily to foreign affairs. In June 1969 Nixon announced that he would begin a phased withdrawal of American forces. In April 1970 Nixon announced that United States troops had been sent into Cambodia to seek out and destroy North Vietnamese and Viet Cong supply bases. This extension of the war effort in Indochina in 1970 aroused strong opposition.

In June 1970 Nixon signed into law a bill lowering the voting age in federal elections from 21 to 18. In mid-1971 the 26th Amendment to the Constitution, extending the franchise to citizens 18 years of age in all elections, was ratified.

The Nixon Administration applied pressure to encourage foreign governments to help resolve the international monetary crisis by realigning their currencies. Foreign governments, in turn, urged Nixon to devalue the dollar. This he did in December 1971.

Nixon conducted his campaign for a second term by surrogate and won by a landslide. On Jan. 27, 1973 Nixon welcomed home the last American ground troops and prisoners of war from Vietnam. American military involvement continued with bombing raids over Cambodia until mid-August.

A major issue at the beginning of Nixon's second term became known as the Watergate scandal. In June 1972, agents hired by the Committee for the Reelection of the President had been arrested while breaking into the Democratic National Committee headquarters at the Watergate apartment-office complex in Washington, D.C. The Senate held hearings to probe allegations of attempts by high White House officials to cover up administration involvement in the case.

Meanwhile, the House Judiciary Committee began an inquiry into whether he had committed impeachable offenses. Three tapes studied in criminal proceedings documented Nixon's personal order to cover up the Watergate break-in. The House Judiciary Committee had already voted in late July to recommend Nixon's impeachment. With Congressional support destroyed, Nixon chose to resign. Gerald

Ford succeeded him on Aug. 9, 1974. Within a month Ford granted Nixon a full pardon for all crimes he may have committed during his administration.

Nixon spent the next 20 years trying to rehabilitate his domestic reputation, though he never lost the admiration of foreign leaders. He became a respected elder statesman in foreign affairs. Nixon died on April 22, 1994, in a New York City hospital, four days after suffering a severe stroke.

KWAME NKRUMAH

(b. 1909 – d. 1972)

One of the outstanding leaders in the African struggles against colonialism in the 1950s was Kwame Nkrumah. He became the first president of independent Ghana and later established a one-party dictatorship.

Nkrumah was born in Nkroful, Gold Coast, in September 1909. He graduated from Achimota College in 1930 and taught in Roman Catholic schools and at a seminary. His interest in religion was deflected by the politics of African nationalism in about 1934. He went to the United States in 1935 and studied at Lincoln University in Pennsylvania. After graduation in 1939 he earned master's degrees from Lincoln and the University of Pennsylvania. Politically Nkrumah was a Marxist-socialist. After studying at the London School of Economics, Nkrumah returned home in 1947 and became a spokesman in the United Gold Coast Convention to work for self-government. In 1950 he initiated a program of nonviolent noncooperation against British rule.

In 1951 Nkrumah was elected to Parliament, and in 1952 he became prime minister. When the Gold Coast and British Togoland became independent as the nation of Ghana in 1957, his party controlled the legislature. In 1960 he was named president and in 1964 became president for life. His rule, which lasted until a military coup ousted him on Feb. 24, 1966, was authoritarian, and his economic policies were a total failure. He went into exile in Guinea and died in Bucharest, Romania, on April 27, 1972.

JULIUS NYERERE

(b. 1922 – d. 1999)

The first prime minister of an independent Tanganyika, Julius Nyerere was also a leader in the founding of the Organization of African Unity in 1963. A year later he became the first president of the new state of Tanzania, a merger of Tanganyika with the island of Zanzibar.

Julius Kambarage Nyerere was born in 1922 in Butiama, Tanganyika. He was educated at schools in Uganda, and he taught in several Roman Catholic schools before going to Scotland to earn a degree at the University of Edinburgh in 1952. He entered politics when Tanganyika was under a United Nations mandate waiting for independence. From 1954 until 1960, as leader of the Tanganyika African National Union, he worked with British authorities to prepare for independence. The country finally obtained self-government in September 1960, and in December 1961 Nyerere became the first prime minister. A year later he was elected president, and in 1964 the union of Zanzibar and Tanganyika was affected. He installed a one-party government on the grounds that a new country struggling to build its economy cannot be threatened with political divisions and frequent elections. Although there was much criticism of his policies, which left his country dependent on international aid, they did create a high literacy rate, unite Tanzanians across ethnic lines, and leave the country relatively untouched by the tensions that troubled other parts of Africa. Nyerere resigned the presidency in 1985 but retained chairmanship of the party until 1990.

As a major force in the formation of the Organization of African Unity, Nyerere was a key figure in African events in the 1970s. He was a strong advocate of the destruction of the white-supremacist regimes in South Africa and in Rhodesia (now Zimbabwe). His army was instrumental in the overthrow of Uganda's dictator Idi Amin in 1979. This intervention helped restore Milton Obote to power.

For all his support of a strong central government in Tanzania, Nyerere opposed nationalism and embraced the concept of African unity

121

as the means to economic development. The Lusaka Manifesto, which he helped formulate, called for cooperation among the races in developing the continent. Nyerere died on Oct. 14, 1999, in London, England.

BARACK OBAMA

(b. 1961–)

I n only four years Barack Obama made an improbable rise from the state legislature of Illinois to the highest office of the United States. The first black American to win the presidency, he made history with his resounding victory in the election of 2008.

Barack Hussein Obama II was born on August 4, 1961, in Honolulu,

Hawaii. After high school in Honolulu, Obama attended Occidental College in Los Angeles and Columbia University in New York City, where he received a bachelor's degree in political science in 1983. Obama worked as a business writer before becoming a community organizer in Chicago in 1985. Three years later he entered Harvard Law School. While working at a Chicago law firm in the summer of 1989, Obama met Chicago native Michelle Robinson, a young lawyer at the firm. The two married in 1992 and had two daughters, Malia and Sasha.

U.S. President Barack Obama, delivering remarks in the White House rose garden in 2011. Jewel Samad/AFP/Getty Images

After law school Obama returned to Chicago and

became active in the Democratic Party. He also practiced civil rights law and taught constitutional law at the University of Chicago. Obama's first book, the memoir *Dreams from My Father*, was released in 1995 to little fanfare, although it received generally positive reviews.

In 1996 Obama was elected as a Democrat to the Illinois Senate, where he would serve for eight years. As a state senator he helped pass legislation that tightened campaign finance regulations, expanded health care to poor families, and reformed criminal justice and welfare laws.

In 2004 Obama ran for a seat in the U.S. Senate. He was only the third African American to be elected to the Senate since the end of Reconstruction in 1877. While campaigning for the Senate, Obama became one of the most talked-about young politicians in a generation. His keynote address at the Democratic National Convention in July 2004 instantly made him a political superstar.

After taking office as a senator in 2005, Obama quickly became a major figure in his party. He received several coveted committee assignments, including a post on the Foreign Relations Committee and Environment and Public Works committees. Obama achieved a level of visibility that was rare for a first-term senator.

In early 2007 Obama declared himself in the running for the 2008 Democratic presidential nomination. The overwhelming favorite to win the nomination was Sen. Hillary Clinton of New York. However, Obama's personal charisma, stirring oratory, and campaign promise to bring change to the political system won him the support of many Democrats, especially young and minority voters.

Obama officially accepted the nomination at the Democratic National Convention in August, becoming the first African American to be nominated for the presidency by either major party. He chose Joe Biden, a longtime senator from Delaware, as his vice presidential running mate. A key issue in the hard-fought campaign was the Iraq War, with Obama calling for a swift withdrawal of most U.S. forces from Iraq.

In the weeks leading up to the election, the recent collapse of some of the largest U.S. banks and financial institutions made the economy the single most important issue. The economic meltdown propelled Obama's campaign, which called the crisis a result of the policies of outgoing Republican President George W. Bush.

In November 2008 Obama decisively won the presidency, capturing 365 electoral votes and some 53 percent of the popular vote. In addition to being the first African American president, he was also the first sitting U.S. senator to win the office since John F. Kennedy in 1960. He was inaugurated as president on January 20, 2009.

In his first months in office, Obama worked to restore the international image of the United States. He ordered the closing of the controversial military detention facility in Guantánamo Bay, Cuba, within a year (a deadline that was not met). In June 2009 he traveled to the Middle East and gave a speech calling for a new relationship between the United States and the Muslim world. In recognition of such efforts, Obama was awarded the 2009 Nobel Prize for Peace.

Obama's top domestic priority was the ongoing economic recession. Aided by Democratic majorities in both the Senate and the House of Representatives, Obama pushed through Congress a massive stimulus package that pumped hundreds of billions of dollars into the struggling economy. By late 2009 the stimulus had reversed the dramatic decline in the gross domestic product. Despite these gains, however, unemployment remained high, and Republicans complained that the stimulus had been too costly.

A sweeping financial reform bill passed in July 2010 was another response to the recession. The bill empowered the government to take over and shut down large troubled financial firms and created a council of federal regulators to monitor the financial system, among other provisions. The passage of the bill was a major legislative victory for the president.

Another early priority of Obama's presidency was reforming the country's health care system. Obama had called for reforms that would make health care insurance more affordable and extend coverage to tens of millions of Americans who lacked it. The issue provoked a prolonged and sometimes bitter debate, with Republicans complaining that Democratic proposals constituted a costly "government takeover" of health care.

In late 2009 the Democratic-controlled House of Representatives and Senate each passed a version of the health care bill. In March 2010, as the historic measure teetered on the brink of defeat, Obama and other Democratic leaders mounted a last-ditch campaign to pass it. The president became more forceful in promoting the bill, both to Congress and to the American people. Later that month Congress passed the bill with no Republican support.

Obama's key foreign-policy challenges were the ongoing wars in Iraq and Afghanistan. Throughout the presidential campaign he had argued that the focus of U.S. military efforts should be in Afghanistan rather than Iraq. In keeping with this philosophy, Obama set an 18-month timetable for the withdrawal of U.S. combat troops from Iraq and in August 2010, on schedule, the U.S. combat mission in Iraq ended. On May 1, 2011, he announced that U.S. Special Forces had killed Osama bin Laden, leader of the terrorist group al-Qaeda, in a firefight in a compound in Abbottabad, Pakistan.

Obama officially kicked off his bid for reelection in May 2012. His Republican opponent was Mitt Romney, a former governor of Massachusetts. Romney spent much of his campaign criticizing Obama's handling of the economy, but the Republicans' effort fell short. On November 6, 2012, Obama was reelected for a second term as president.

THE PERÓNS

Juan Perón (b. 1895–d. 1974)
Eva Perón (b. 1919–d. 1952)

Although Juan Perón of Argentina was one of the more remarkable and charismatic Latin American politicians of the 20th century, he may eventually be remembered because of his marriage to the talented and shrewd Eva Duarte. It was she who became the center of a powerful personality cult that endured after her death. A television drama was based on her life, and she is the subject of the long-running stage musical *Evita*.

Juan Domingo Perón was born to a lower middle-class family in the province of Buenos Aires on Oct. 8, 1895. He entered military school at age 16 and made the army his career. In the 1930s he served as a military expert on Argentina's diplomatic staff in Italy, which gave him the chance to observe Benito Mussolini's Fascist government. Back in Argentina in 1943, he joined a group plotting to overthrow the civilian government. He held several government posts but was ousted and imprisoned in October 1945. On October 17 he announced his candidacy for the presidency after Eva rallied support for his release.

She was born María Eva Duarte on May 7, 1919, at Los Toldos near Buenos Aires. By the time she met Perón she had become a popular radio and film actress. They were married in late October 1945.

Perón was elected in 1946 with 56 percent of the vote. During his first term Eva became a powerful, but unofficial, influence revered by the lower classes as Evita. She organized woman workers, obtained for women the right to vote, promoted welfare programs, and introduced compulsory religious education. Perón nationalized the railroads and other utilities and financed public works. He used the armed forces to stifle dissent.

He was reelected by a large margin in 1951. On July 26, 1952, Eva Perón died of cancer. On Sept. 19, 1955, he was overthrown by a group of officers opposed to the corruption and oppression of his rule. He settled in Madrid, Spain, and in 1961 married a dancer known as Isabel Martínez. She was born María Estela Martínez Cartas in La Rioja, Argentina, on Feb. 4, 1931.

Perón's followers, known as Peronistas, remained a strong force in Argentine politics. No regime after Perón's was able to solve the country's economic problems. In March 1973 Peronista candidates captured the presidency, and Perón returned to a tumultuous welcome. He was elected president, and his wife became vice president. He died on July 1, 1974, and she assumed his office. She failed to win the type of support Eva had received, and on March 24, 1976, she was ousted by the armed forces.

PETER THE GREAT

(b. 1672–d. 1725)

The founder of the Russian Empire was Peter I, called Peter the Great. Under him, Russia ceased to be a poor and backward Asian country and became a modern power in the Western European world.

Peter was born near Moscow on May 30, 1672, according to the Old Style calendar, or on June 9, according to the New Style. His father, Czar Alexis I Mikhailovich, died before Peter was 4. Peter's half-brother Fyodor, who then became czar, died in 1682. Peter and another half-brother, Ivan, were to rule jointly, but because Ivan was sickly and mentally retarded, his sister Sophia served as regent. Peter, excluded from the government, grew up in a village outside Moscow. His mother had had the benefit of a progressive education, and her influence and Peter's freedom from the limitations of court life helped him to develop his natural intelligence and abilities as a leader.

In 1689 Peter wrested power from Sophia. He had been interested since childhood in ships and sailing. He was determined to give Russia an outlet to the sea, both on the Baltic Sea, which was controlled by Sweden, and on the Caspian Sea, whose shores were held by the Turks and Tatars. He brought European shipbuilders to Russia, and in 1696, with a new fleet, was able to capture Azov, the chief Turkish fortress on the Sea of Azov. As Capt. Peter Alekseevich he commanded from the *Principium*, a ship built by his own hand. Peter sent a grand embassy to the European powers in 1697 to enlist their help against Turkey. He went along, pretending to be a ship's carpenter named Peter Mikhailov, and worked in English and Dutch shipyards. He studied everything from anatomy and engraving to European industrial techniques.

Recalled home by a revolt, he set about reorganizing his army. By 1700 he felt ready to attack Sweden. With Poland and Denmark as allies, he started the Great Northern War, which lasted until 1721. In 1703 he built a new capital, St. Petersburg, on territory that he had won.

The Treaty of Nystad (1721) brought the war to an end and gave Russia the prized Swedish provinces on the eastern shores of the Baltic Sea. As a result of the victory the Russian Empire was formed on Oct. 22 (Nov. 2, in New Style), 1721. On that day Peter was acclaimed Father of the Fatherland, Peter the Great, and emperor of all the Russians.

Peter meanwhile introduced many reforms in his backward country. He put a high tax on beards and Oriental dress to force the people to adopt Western dress. He freed women from forced seclusion. He modernized the calendar, simplified the alphabet, unified the currency, and introduced universal taxation. Russia's first modern hospitals and medical schools were built by Peter. He encouraged the rise of private industry and the expansion of trade.

These reforms caused dissatisfaction among the conservatives. Peter's son, Alexis, was tortured and died because he joined the conspirators against his father's rule. In 1712 Peter had married his mistress, a peasant girl named Catherine. He shocked the country by making her his empress. When he died on Jan. 28 (Feb. 8, in New Style), 1725, she succeeded him as Catherine I.

AUGUSTO PINOCHET

(b. 1915–d. 2006)

From the time of his seizure of power in Chile by a military coup in 1973, the name of Gen. Augusto Pinochet was nearly synonymous with rightist, anti-revolutionary politics throughout South America. His supporters, both in Chile and abroad, revered Pinochet as the man who saved Chile from the economic collapse begun during the presidency of socialist leader Salvador Allende. His opponents, with equal vehemence, accused General Pinochet of seizing power undemocratically, snuffing out all traces of political opposition, and subjecting Chile to nearly two decades of authoritarian rule.

Augusto Pinochet Ugarte was born in Valparaíso, Chile, on Nov. 15, 1915. A graduate of the military academy in Santiago (1936), Pinochet became a career military officer and was appointed army commander in chief by President Allende before a military junta overthrew Allende's government in 1973. Pinochet was named head of the victorious junta's governing council, and he moved to crush Chile's liberal opposition; in its first three years, the regime arrested approximately 130,000, many of whom were tortured. In June 1974 Pinochet assumed sole power as president, relegating the rest of the junta to an advisory role. Under Pinochet's regime, political terror, repression of human rights, and intolerance of criticism of the government remained constant features.

Immediately after seizing power, Pinochet cut off diplomatic relations with Cuba. This suspension of relations with Cuba marked a symbolic and decisive shift away from the socialist policies of Allende's rule.

While Pinochet maintained some of the land reforms of the Allende era, he quickly moved to restore free-market economic policies to the Chilean government. In addition, hundreds of industries that had been nationalized during the Allende era were returned to their previous owners.

Gen. Augusto Pinochet, watching U.S. planes fly over Chile's El Bosque air base. Marco Ugarte/AFP/Getty Images

The return of numerous major industries to their original United States owners, as well as the crackdown on leftists in Chile, led to widespread speculation that the military coup had been conducted with the support of the United States government. While Pinochet denied these allegations, evidence quickly surfaced that the United States had in fact pumped millions of dollars into the anti-Allende camp with the intent to destabilize Allende's socialist government. Following the coup, United States President Richard Nixon, a staunch anti-Communist, openly embraced Pinochet's regime. The United States removed economic sanctions that had been put into place following Allende's election, and billions of dollars worth of aid were funneled into the Chilean economy.

With the firm backing of the United States, Pinochet successfully engineered an economic recovery. While keeping an authoritarian grip on public life, Pinochet simultaneously withdrew government control over industry and agriculture. Inflation was reigned in. As a result of these free-market policies, the Chilean economy grew steadily throughout the late 1970s and early 1980s. However much of the burden for this economic recovery was placed on the backs of the working classes and rural poor, essentially marking a return to the sharp social divisions of the pre-Allende days.

Under a new constitution spread in March 1981, Pinochet remained president for an eight-year term until 1989, when a national referendum would determine whether he would serve an additional eight-year term. Pinochet permitted no meaningful political opposition, but he fulfilled his constitutional obligation to hold the vote, which took place earlier than mandated in October 1988. The result was a "no" vote of 55 percent and a "yes" vote of 43 percent. Although rejected by the electorate, Pinochet remained in office until free elections installed a new president in March 11, 1990.

Despite his willingness to abandon the presidency, Pinochet refused to turn absolute authority over to a civilian government. Pinochet exercised his constitutional right to keep his post as the head of the armed forces, despite calls from opposition candidates for his resignation. Despite his diminished power, Pinochet—as the leader of the influential Chilean army—remained a powerful behind-the-scenes figure in Chile until his official retirement from the military in March 1998. Following his retirement from the military, Pinochet received a permanent post in the Chilean senate, ignoring calls from his opponents that he be barred from participating in democratic institutions.

In October 1998, while visiting London, Pinochet was detained by British authorities after Spain requested his extradition in connection with the torture of Spanish citizens in Chile during his rule. The unprecedented case stirred worldwide controversy and galvanized human-rights organizations in Chile. Many countries released formerly classified documents concerning Chileans who were kidnapped and presumably killed by the Pinochet regime. In January 2000 Pinochet was allowed to return home after a British court ruled that he was physically unfit to stand trial. Nevertheless, he continued to face investigations by Chilean authorities.

In 2001 Pinochet was stripped of his immunity from prosecution—which he had enjoyed as a former president—and ordered to stand trial on charges of human-rights abuses. The charges were dropped in 2002, however, after Chile's Supreme Court upheld a ruling that he was mentally incapable of defending himself in court. Soon afterward Pinochet resigned his post as a senator-for-life. In 2005 he was again stripped of immunity and ordered to stand trial. Before prosecutors could try him, however, Pinochet died on Dec. 10, 2006, in Santiago.

POL POT

(b. 1925–d. 1998)

Pol Pot, also called Tol Saut or Pol Porth, was one of the most reviled tyrants of the 20th century. The leader of the Khmer Rouge regime, he was held responsible for the deaths of nearly two million Cambodians during his rule from 1975 to 1979.

Born in 1925 in the Kompong Thom province of Cambodia, Saloth Sar—the man who would eventually take the name Pol Pot—emerged from humble peasant origins to become the leader of Cambodia's radical revolutionary Khmer Rouge party. Like many in the region then known as French Indochina, Saloth Sar began his political career fighting under Vietnamese independence leader Ho Chi Minh in the Indo-Chinese campaign against France.

In 1949, at the age of 20, Saloth Sar left Cambodia and traveled to Paris on scholarship to study radio technology. In Paris, he devoted his time to radical student organizations, becoming further committed to the ideology of Communism, with which he first became acquainted during his period in the anti-French resistance. Following Ho Chi Minh and Chinese peasant Communist revolutionary leader Mao Zedong, Saloth Sar came to embrace a radical political ideology that blended aspects of rural-based Marxism with the dogma of nationalism.

Pol Pot returned to Cambodia in 1953 to find a country far different from the one he had left only four years before. French rule was on the verge of collapse throughout Indochina, and Cambodia had received limited autonomy under the French. The following year, Cambodia won full independence following France's defeat in its war with Indochina, and an independent state was established under the Cambodian royal dynasty of King Norodom Sihanouk. Saloth Sar secretly worked in the Cambodian radical underground to foment opposition to the monarchy of King Sihanouk.

In 1960, Saloth Sar, along with other Cambodian Communists, formed the Cambodian Communist Party. King Sihanouk later dubbed this group the "Khmer Rouge," or Red Cambodians, a name that the party itself embraced. As a leader of this movement, Saloth Sar took the pseudonym Pol Pot. In 1967, with Pol Pot firmly in charge of the organization, the Khmer Rouge began its military campaign against the Cambodian government, using guerrilla tactics developed and honed by Mao Zedong and Ho Chi Minh.

For 15 years the Khmer Rouge waged a prolonged war against the Cambodian governments of King Norodom Sihanouk and, after Sihanouk was deposed in 1970, the United States–supported government of military general Lon Nol. In 1975, following the withdrawal of United States forces from neighboring Vietnam, the Khmer Rouge attacked and invaded the Cambodian capital of Phnom Penh, bringing the country under its control. From 1975 to 1979, the Khmer Rouge governed the country with a ruthless and bloody hand. Nearly two million Cambodians were killed during the four-year experiment in peasant Communism. Many died from starvation and disease during the Khmer Rouge government's attempt to collectivize agricultural production. Even more were killed by direct methods as the Khmer Rouge conducted purges of its own ranks and willfully tortured and executed political opponents and so-called class enemies.

In 1979, conflicts between Cambodia and Vietnam led to a Vietnamese invasion. The Vietnamese army deposed Pol Pot's government and established a puppet government in its place. The Khmer Rouge fled to neighboring Thailand and, with the backing of the Thai government, established military bases on the southern Thai border. For 17 years the Khmer Rouge continued to fight against the various Cambodian governments, despite the fact that a supposed peace agreement was signed between all warring factions in 1991.

Elections in 1993, which were boycotted by the Khmer Rouge, brought Norodom Ranaridah, the son of King Sihanouk, to power in a coalition government. In August 1996 the government announced that it would offer amnesty to any Khmer Rouge guerrillas who left Pol Pot's army and joined the government's forces. Approximately 4,000 members of the Khmer Rouge, led by Pol Pot's brother-in-law, accepted the government's offer, leaving fewer than 4,000 guerrillas under the command of Pol Pot.

These last vestiges of the once-powerful Khmer Rouge peasant army began to split apart, siding with the various rivals for power within the

Khmer Rouge hierarchy and ultimately leading to the fall of Pol Pot in 1997. Unconfirmed reports stated that sharp disagreements had broken out between a Khmer Rouge faction loyal to Pol Pot and one loyal to his former defense minister, Son Sen. The power struggle between the two men culminated in Pol Pot's allegedly ordering the execution of Son Sen and 11 members of Son Sen's family on June 16, 1997. Following the executions, a 1,000-man force loyal to Son Sen turned against Pol Pot and pursued him and 300 loyal soldiers deep into the thick Cambodian jungle. After five days of pursuit, Pol Pot, ailing and abandoned by all but 15 soldiers, was apprehended by his former allies on the Cambodia-Thailand border.

Following the capture of Pol Pot, the Cambodian government wanted to have the former dictator tried by an international tribunal. The United States, which had been directly involved in the struggle against Pol Pot's forces in the 1970s, backed the Cambodian government's proposal to capture Pol Pot and try him before a world court on charges of genocide. However, the former dictator, held under house arrest by the Khmer Rouge, died of an apparent heart attack on April 15, 1998, before he could be brought to trial.

VLADIMIR PUTIN

(b. 1952–)

In an announcement that surprised the locals and the world, Russia's President Boris Yeltsin resigned on Dec. 31, 1999. Yeltsin left in his place a relatively unknown Vladimir Putin, whom Yeltsin had elevated to the post of prime minister a scant five months earlier. A career foreign intelligence officer by background, Putin was described as austere, reserved, and disciplined.

Vladimir Vladimirovich Putin was born on Oct. 7, 1952, in Leningrad, U.S.S.R. (now St. Petersburg, Russia). He studied law at Leningrad State University, where his tutor was Anatoli Sobchak, later one of the leading reform politicians of the perestroika period. Putin spent 15 years as a foreign intelligence officer for the Committee for State Security (KGB), including six years in Dresden, East Germany (now Germany).

133

In 1990 he retired from active KGB service with the rank of lieutenant colonel and returned to Russia to become prorector of Leningrad State University with responsibility for the institution's external relations. Soon afterward, Putin became an adviser to Sobchak, the first democratically elected mayor of St. Petersburg. He quickly won Sobchak's confidence and became known for his ability to get things done; by 1994 he had risen to the post of first deputy mayor.

In 1996 Putin moved to Moscow, where he joined the presidential staff as deputy to Pavel Borodin, the Kremlin's chief administrator. Putin grew close to fellow Leningrader Anatoli Chubais and moved up in administrative positions. In July 1998 President Yeltsin made Putin director of the Federal Security Service (the KGB's domestic successor), and shortly thereafter he became secretary of the influential Security Council. Yeltsin, who was searching for an heir to assume his position, appointed Putin prime minister in 1999.

As prime minister, the virtually unknown Putin saw his public-approval ratings soar when he launched a well-organized military operation against the secessionist rebels in Chechnya. Wearied by years of Yeltsin's erratic behavior, the population appreciated Putin's coolness and decisiveness under pressure. Putin's support for the new electoral bloc, Unity, ensured its success in the December parliamentary elections. On December 31, Yeltsin unexpectedly announced his resignation and named Putin acting president.

Promising to rebuild a weakened Russia, Putin easily won the March 2000 elections with about 53 percent of the vote. As president, Putin sought to end corruption and create a strongly regulated free-market economy. He faced a difficult situation in Chechnya, where the rebels proved to be unexpectedly tenacious; in 2002 Putin declared the military campaign over, but casualties remained high.

Overseeing an economy that enjoyed growth after a prolonged recession in the 1990s, Putin was easily reelected in March 2004. In parliamentary elections in December 2007, Putin's party, United Russia, won an overwhelming majority of seats. A constitutional provision forced Putin to step down in 2008. His chosen successor, Dmitry Medvedev, won the March 2008 presidential election by a landslide. Putin again ran for presidential elections in 2012, and won amidst widespread demonstrations against him as well as allegations of poll fraud and vote rigging.

MUAMMAR AL-QADDAFI

(b. 1942–d. 2011)

On Sept. 1, 1969, King Idris I of Libya was overthrown in a blood-less military coup. The leader of the coup was a 27-year-old army captain, Muammar al-Qaddafi, who seized control of the government and made himself Libya's new ruler.

Qaddafi was born in 1942 near Surt, Libya, to desert Bedouins. The transliteration of his name from Arabic into English varies. His own preference is Gadhafi; another spelling is Khadafy. During secondary school he was already plotting the overthrow of the government. His hero and model was Egypt's revolutionary leader Gamal Abdel Nasser. Qaddafi graduated from the University of Libya in 1963 and from the military academy at Banghazi in 1965. By the time he attained the rank of captain in 1969, he and fellow officers had developed a plan to control Libya.

After overthrowing the king, Qaddafi took control of the government and became a colonel and commander in chief of the armed forces. He came to rule with his own blend of strict Islamic principles and socialism, a system that he outlined in *The Green Book* (1976–80). He nationalized foreign-owned petroleum assets and banks and confiscated the property of Italians and Jews living in Libya. Revenues from petroleum exports were used to build industrial plants, highways, hospitals, and irrigation projects.

After Nasser's death in 1970 Qaddafi regarded himself as the leader of the Arab world. A strong proponent of Arab nationalism, he persistently tried to merge Libya with other Arab countries. He interfered in the affairs of neighboring nations, notably Chad, where he tried to gain control. He sponsored terrorist activities around the world, including the training of terrorists to fight Israel. He was strongly opposed to the United States because of its support for Israel.

In April 1986, in response to Libya's alleged terrorist activities in Europe, the United States bombed sites in Tripoli and Banghazi, including Qaddafi's residence. Qaddafi narrowly escaped, but one of his daughters was killed. Qaddafi was further isolated from the international community after his government was purportedly involved in the bombing of a civilian airliner over Lockerbie, Scotland, in 1988. Both the UN and United States instituted economic sanctions against Libya.

Qaddafi later worked to repair his global image and to improve Libya's relations with the West. In 1999 he turned over the suspects in the Lockerbie bombing to international authorities for trial, and in 2003 he agreed to halt Libya's program to develop unconventional weapons. Most of the sanctions against Libya were dropped in 2003.

His attempts to unify Arab countries having failed, Qaddafi began to emphasize African unity and helped to found the African Union in 2000. He was elected its chairman in 2009.

In February 2011, after antigovernment demonstrations forced the presidents of the neighboring countries of Tunisia and Egypt from power, anti-Qaddafi demonstrations broke out in the Libyan city of Banghazi. As the protests spread throughout the country, the Qaddafi regime attempted to violently suppress them, firing live ammunition at protesters and attacking them. Foreign government officials and international human rights groups condemned the regime's assault on the protesters.

Qaddafi's hold on power appeared increasingly weak as the opposition forces gained strength. By the end of February, opposition forces had established control over large amounts of Libyan territory, encircling Tripoli, where Qaddafi remained in control but in growing isolation.

In August 2011 Qaddafi's hold on power appeared to break when rebel forces entered and took control of most areas of Tripoli. They achieved a major symbolic victory on August 23 when they captured Qaddafi's headquarters in Tripoli. Jubilant crowds ransacked the compound, destroying symbols of the Qaddafi regime.

Qaddafi's whereabouts remained uncertain, although he released several audio messages urging the Libyan people to resist the rebels. As rebel forces solidified their hold on Tripoli, they intensified their efforts to track down Qaddafi, offering a $1.7 million reward for killing or capturing him. Qaddafi was killed in Surt on October 20 as rebel forces took control of the city, one of the last remaining loyalist strongholds.

RONALD W. REAGAN

(b. 1911–d. 2004)

I n a stunning electoral landslide, Ronald Reagan was elected the 40th president of the United States in 1980. "The Great Communicator," as he was sometimes called, was considered to be the most conservative candidate to win the office in half a century.

Ronald Wilson Reagan was born on Feb. 6, 1911, in Tampico, Ill. In high school and college Reagan showed his ability in the three fields that came to dominate his life—sports, drama, and politics.

Reagan was contracted to the Warner Brothers studio in 1937. During the following 27 years he appeared in more than 50 movies. While filming *Brother Rat* in 1938, Reagan met Jane Wyman, another Warners contract player. Married in 1940, they had a daughter and adopted a son. The two divorced in 1948.

Between 1947 and 1960 Reagan served six terms as president of the Screen Actors Guild, the union of movie actors. He helped achieve better pay, revised tax procedures, and improved working conditions for actors.

Militantly anti-Communist, Reagan appeared in 1947 as a cooperative witness before the House Committee on Un-American Activities, which was investigating Communist influence in the movie industry. In 1952 Reagan married actress Nancy Davis. They had a son and a daughter together.

U.S. President Ronald Reagan, donning a hat during a meeting with American Olympic athletes at the White House in 1988. AFP/ Getty Images

137

Initially a liberal Democrat, Reagan's political opinions gradually grew more conservative. In 1962 he officially switched his registration to the Republican Party. With the support of businessmen and other conservative backers Reagan entered the 1966 race for the governorship of California. He conducted a campaign on such issues as welfare, student dissidents, crime, and "big government." Reagan won by nearly a million votes. He was reelected in 1970.

Several of Reagan's accomplishments during his terms as governor were highly regarded, even by his political opponents. He doubled aid to schools and increased expenditures for mental health by 400 percent. He cooperated with the legislature in reforming the state's welfare system by restricting eligibility and reducing the number of people receiving benefits, while increasing benefits for the most needy.

In 1968, while serving his first term as governor of California, Reagan announced his candidacy for president during the Republican convention. He did not win the nomination that year and narrowly lost it in 1976. By May 1980 Reagan had enough delegates to win the nomination. On election day, Reagan defeated Carter and John Anderson with slightly more than half the popular vote. At age 69, Reagan was the oldest person to be elected president.

The first months of Reagan's presidency were dramatic. Just after his inauguration he announced that Iran had agreed to release the American hostages who had been held captive at the U.S. Embassy in Tehran since November 1979. He also survived an assassination attempt.

From the beginning of his presidency Reagan tried to reduce the role of the federal government. He proposed massive tax cuts and increased defense spending as well as significant reductions in spending on social-welfare programs such as education, food stamps, and low-income housing.

A severe recession in 1982 lessened the appeal of so-called Reaganomics. To address the deficit problem, Reagan made a policy reversal and supported a tax increase in 1982. By early 1983 the economy had begun to recover, and by the end of that year unemployment and inflation were significantly reduced. The strong recovery aided Reagan's landslide reelection in 1984. Economic growth continued through the remainder of Reagan's presidency.

In foreign policy Reagan took an early stand against the Soviet Union. In 1983 he announced his Strategic Defense Initiative, a space-based missile defense system popularly called Star Wars. Historic summits between Reagan and Soviet leader Mikhail Gorbachev in 1985, 1986, and 1987 resulted in a treaty reducing intermediate-range nuclear weapons.

In 1986 Reagan became embroiled in the worst scandal of his political career. Late in the year the public discovered that his administration had secretly sold weapons to Iran in exchange for that country's help in securing the release of American hostages held by terrorists in Lebanon. This violated a U.S. policy that prohibited relations with countries—such as Iran—that supported terrorism. Soon it was revealed that profits from the sale had been illegally diverted to the *contras* in Nicaragua.

Senate hearings on what was called the Iran-*contra* affair began in 1987. By 1990 six former Reagan officials had been convicted in the affair. Reagan accepted responsibility for the arms-for-hostages deal but denied any knowledge of the diversion of the profits to the *contras*.

After years of declining health, Reagan revealed in 1994 that he had been diagnosed with Alzheimer's disease. He died on June 5, 2004, in Los Angeles, Calif.

MAXIMILIEN DE ROBESPIERRE

(b. 1758–d. 1794)

One of the leaders of the French Revolution during its Reign of Terror was Robespierre. His humanity in his early years was in strange contrast to his cruelty and intolerance during the revolution.

Maximilien de Robespierre was born on May 6, 1758, in Arras and studied law in Arras and in Paris. As a lawyer in his native city, he was noted for his ability and honesty. He resigned as a judge rather than pronounce a sentence of death and tried to abolish the death penalty.

Robespierre was a great admirer of the philosopher Jean-Jacques Rousseau. At the approach of the revolution he saw an opportunity to establish the ideal society that Rousseau envisioned.

In 1789 Robespierre was a delegate to the Estates-General, the representative assembly that was then meeting for the first time in

175 years. He quickly became the leader of that body and head of the powerful Jacobin Club. This was an extremist group that advocated exile or death for the nobility and royalty.

Paris mobs stormed the palace of the Tuileries in 1792 and dethroned King Louis XVI and his queen, Marie Antoinette. Robespierre helped organize the new revolutionary governing body, the Commune of Paris. With his skill as an orator, he demanded the execution of the king and queen. He soon got his wish: the king was executed in January 1793 and the queen nearly ten months later.

The following year the Committee of Public Safety took over the rule of the country to suppress royalist uprisings and to repel the Prussian-Austrian invaders on its borders. The bloody three-year rule of this body was known as the Reign of Terror. Robespierre, Georges Danton, and Jean-Paul Marat were the most powerful members.

Robespierre was not entirely to blame for the excesses of the Committee of Public Safety. He was not a man of action. He rarely attended its sessions and had almost no part in its routine work. His love of power and narrow self-righteousness, however, made him feared and hated by many of his associates. He sent to the guillotine Jacques-René Hébert, an atheist who had closed the churches and set up a grotesque worship of "the goddess Reason." Robespierre introduced the Reign of Virtue and the worship of "the Supreme Being." He had Danton guillotined for urging moderation and an end of the Reign of Terror.

On July 27, 1794, Robespierre's enemies had him arrested. In the confusion that followed an attempted rescue, part of his jaw was shot away. The next day he and 19 of his followers were guillotined—a fulfillment of Danton's words, "Robespierre will follow me; I drag down Robespierre." With his fall the terror soon ended.

FRANKLIN DELANO ROOSEVELT

(b. 1882–d. 1945)

Everyone had strong feelings about Franklin D. Roosevelt during his 12 years as president. As president, Roosevelt used his powers to

FRANKLIN DELANO ROOSEVELT

create jobs in a world-wide business depression. During World War II he was the real commander in chief of the American armed forces. He took charge of the industrial might of the country. He also played a major part in setting up the United Nations.

Roosevelt was born Jan. 30, 1882, near Hyde Park, N.Y. He studied at Harvard University and then Columbia University Law School in New York City. He completed his work in 1907 and began to practice with a leading New York law firm.

Meanwhile, on March

Franklin Delano Roosevelt, photographed during one of his Fireside Chat radio addresses while president of the United States. Library of Congress Prints and Photographs Division

17, 1905, he married Anna Eleanor Roosevelt, his sixth cousin. President Theodore Roosevelt, her uncle, came to New York City to give the bride away. In the next ten years the Roosevelts had six children.

In 1910 the Democratic Party helped nominate him for state senator, and he won by a narrow margin. In 1913 he became assistant secretary of the navy in Woodrow Wilson's government. From 1913 to 1921 Roosevelt was a tireless assistant to secretary of the navy. When the United States went to war in 1917, its need for men in the war was met, partly through Roosevelt's efforts.

When Roosevelt and his family were at Campobello for a vacation he went to bed with what he thought was a bad cold and found that polio (infantile paralysis) gripped him. After days of pain and fever, he was left with the aftereffects of the disease—his legs were completely and permanently paralyzed. However, polio did not stop him; he exercised hard and got his strength back.

He later ran for governor of New York in 1928. Roosevelt's governorship was not spectacular, but he was reelected in 1930 by a large margin of 725,000 votes. The victory turned all eyes on him as a possible president.

The stock-market crash of 1929 threw the nation's economic system into disorder. Many people searched for a new leader. Roosevelt's vigorous relief policies convinced them he was on their side. The presidential campaign of 1932 was staged against the background of the depression. At the polls Roosevelt won all but six states with a massive margin.

In the winter of 1932–33 the depression deepened. Industrial production fell to the lowest level ever recorded. The nation seemed paralyzed. On March 4, 1933, Roosevelt's inaugural address did much to restore public confidence. He called for courage, stating that "the only thing we have to fear is fear itself."

Roosevelt then tried to balance the budget. He sanctioned "emergency" spending for relief, recovery, and national defense. With the swift end of the banking crisis and the pledge of government economy, optimism began to return.

Meanwhile the New Deal, the name given Roosevelt's overall plan of action, was taking shape. One part of the program was to promote recovery. Another was to supply relief to the needy. A third part was to furnish permanent reforms, especially in the management of banks and stock exchanges. Congress and the public trusted Roosevelt so completely that a record number of bills were passed in the 99-day session.

In 1935 Roosevelt proposed his social security measures. In his annual message he declared that the day of great private fortunes was ended. Instead, wealth must be better distributed. Every citizen must be guaranteed "a proper security, a reasonable leisure, and a decent living throughout life." It was time for the United States to follow Britain in providing insurance for unemployment and old age.

The Social Security Act was signed August 1935. Under it the unemployed and the aged were to be looked after by combined state and federal action. The national government was also to help the states pay pensions to old people. A separate federal annuity system, based on wage earners' contributions, was to give every contributor a pension at 65.

In 1936 Roosevelt tried for reelection with most big businessmen against him but with most farmers, workmen, and small storekeepers on his side. It was a Roosevelt landslide.

While Congress was passing neutrality laws regarding participation in the ongoing international conflicts, a general European war was about to start. For 27 months the United States was officially neutral. On Sunday, Dec. 7, 1941, Japanese forces made a surprise attack on Pearl Harbor. The United States was in World War II.

In 1942, the U.S. Congress passed the First and Second War Powers acts and other laws that gave Roosevelt full authority. He had control over farming, manufacturing, labor, prices, wages, transportation, and allotment of raw materials. In turn he gave these powers to the right men, boards, or departments. Many war agencies were set up. Shifting and changing as needed, they brought nearly every activity of the country under government direction.

Close to Roosevelt's heart was the formation of a new world organization, more effective than the old League of Nations. On May 30, 1944, the United States invited Britain, the Soviet Union, and China to a Washington conference to discuss world peace. Talks began on August 21. A set of plans was submitted for study and comment by people of all nations. This was the first step in the formation of what became the United Nations.

The next step toward building a world peace organization was to hold a full international meeting and draw up a charter. In February 1945, after his election in 1944 to a fourth term as president, Roosevelt conferred with Churchill and Stalin at Yalta in the Crimea. They discussed final war plans and peace questions.

A meeting was called at San Francisco for April 25, 1945, to put their plan into action. However, on the morning of April 12, 1945, Roosevelt suffered a cerebral hemorrhage and died. He was buried in the garden of his Hyde Park home. The home is now a national historic site.

THEODORE ROOSEVELT

(b. 1858–d. 1919)

T he youngest president of the United States was Theodore Roosevelt. He had been vice president under William McKinley. He came into office in 1901, just before his 43rd birthday. Roosevelt was not only a statesman but a cowboy, soldier, hunter, naturalist, and explorer.

Roosevelt was born on Oct. 27, 1858, at 28 East 20th Street in New York City. From 1876 to 1880 he was a student at Harvard. In his senior year in college Roosevelt fell in love with Alice Lee. They were married after his graduation and went to live in New York City. He attended Columbia Law School. In 1881, when he was only 23 years old, he was elected to the New York State legislature. In spite of his youth he made himself respected, and quickly became known for his opposition to corrupt, party-machine politics. He was easily the leader of the Republicans in the legislature. In 1884 he was chairman of the New York State delegation to the Republican National Convention.

In February 1884 his wife died, two days after the birth of their daughter, Alice. On the same night, in the same house, Roosevelt's mother died. In December 1886 he married his childhood playmate, Edith Carow, in London and settled down to a new life at Sagamore Hill, in Oyster Bay.

In 1895 he took the post of police commissioner in New York City. He tried to put an end to graft and corruption in the police force. He was vigorous and honest, but he did not always use good judgment or diplomacy.

After two years he resigned to accept President McKinley's offer of a post as assistant secretary of the navy. As war with Spain neared, Roosevelt, on his own authority, quietly ordered preparations. He came home to be elected governor of New York in 1898. Those who were closest to him, however, were disturbed by his gift for publicity and his startlingly unconventional approach to politics. Fearing him as a candidate for the presidency, they succeeded in putting him in the post with the most unpromising future—that of vice president of the United States when William McKinley was reelected in 1900. But before the time for the regular session of the Senate, McKinley had been assassinated, shot by a crazed anarchist. Roosevelt then took the oath of office. In 1904, with Charles W. Fairbanks as vice president, he was elected president in his own right by a triumphant majority.

The West always held great interest for Roosevelt. There he had passed happy years on his North Dakota ranch. The conservation of its great forests and its wild life was one of his chief concerns. Acting under a Forest Reserve Act of 1891, he withdrew 150 million acres of timberland from sale, in addition to 85 million acres in Alaska.

He was also active in the international arena. In September 1905, Roosevelt brought about a peace conference between warring Russia and Japan. The conference was held in Portsmouth, N.H. For this service he was awarded the Nobel Peace Prize. In 1906, when France and Germany were ready to fight over their interests in Morocco, Roosevelt took the lead in arranging a conference of the powers in Algeciras, Spain. This meeting temporarily settled the differences.He was also active in planning the Second Hague Peace Conference, where representatives from 44 countries adopted rules governing arbitration.

American prestige was further helped by strengthening the army and navy. Roosevelt pushed Congress hard to get an appropriation for two new battleships a year, and he kept the fleet highly efficient. This was shown by the cruise around the world of 16 battleships, all built since the Spanish-American War. President Roosevelt decided on this cruise in 1907 at a moment when relations between Japan and the United States were strained because of anti-Japanese agitation in California and in Congress. He always regarded it as one of his most important contributions to world peace.

Roosevelt declined to consider a third term and secured the Republican nomination for his friend William H. Taft. He was only 50 years old when he left the White House.

However he could not avoid being drawn back into politics. Friends urged him to be a candidate for president in 1912. He was beaten for the Republican nomination by Taft under circumstances which led to charges of fraud and "steamroller" methods. Roosevelt followers organized the National Progressive Party. He led a gallant fight and made a two months' speaking tour of the country but finished second.

On Jan. 6, 1919, Roosevelt died in his sleep. He was buried near Sagamore Hill. In 1962 his home in Oyster Bay, Long Island, and his boyhood home in New York City were established as national historic sites. His Elkhorn Ranch in North Dakota is part of the Theodore Roosevelt National Memorial Park, which was established in 1947.

ANWAR EL-SADAT

(b. 1918–d. 1981)

The Egyptian soldier and statesman Anwar el-Sadat served as president of Egypt from 1970 until his death. Sadat participated in historic negotiations with Israel that resulted in the signing of a peace treaty and for which he was awarded the Nobel Peace Prize.

Egyptian President Anwar el-Sadat, greeting the crowd at Tel Aviv airport in 1977. AFP/Getty Images

Muhammad Anwar el-Sadat was born on Dec. 25, 1918, in Mit Abu al-Kum, Egypt, a village on the Nile Delta. He attended Muslim schools and graduated from the Cairo Military Academy in 1938. During World War II Sadat collaborated with the Germans to further his goal of ousting the British from Egypt. He was arrested in 1942 for spying, escaped, and was arrested a second time in 1945 for his participation in an assassination attempt. Sadat was released in 1949. When his army command was restored the following year, Sadat joined the Free Officers Movement, an organization pledged to the overthrow of the Egyptian monarchy and led by Gamal

Abdel Nasser. Nasser led a bloodless coup that took power from King Farouk I in 1952.

Sadat held various high positions in the new government, including chairman of the National Assembly from 1960 to 1968 and vice president (1964–66, 1969–70). When Nasser died in 1970, Sadat was elected president with more than 90 percent of the vote in a national referendum.

In 1972 Sadat expelled 15,000 Soviet advisers on the grounds that he was receiving inadequate military support from the Soviet Union. He instigated the Arab-Israeli War of October 1973, when he crossed the Suez Canal to attack Israel. Although Israel counterattacked and established forces on the canal's west bank, Sadat won praise at home and in the Arab world.

At the invitation of Israeli Prime Minister Menachem Begin, Sadat visited Jerusalem in November 1977 and addressed the Knesset, Israel's parliament. In his address Sadat acknowledged Israel's right to exist but called for the return of occupied land and recognition of the rights of Palestinians. For this and for subsequent negotiations, Sadat and Begin shared the Nobel Peace Prize in 1978. Although he was denounced by other Arab leaders, Sadat continued talks and signed a peace treaty with Israel on March 26, 1979.

Sadat faced increasing domestic unrest stemming from opposition to the peace treaty and a failing economy. He was assassinated by Muslim fundamentalists in Cairo on Oct. 6, 1981, while reviewing a military parade that marked the eighth anniversary of the crossing of the Suez Canal.

SADDAM HUSSEIN

(b. 1937–d. 2006)

As president of Iraq from 1979 to 2003, Saddam Hussein was a brutal and warlike ruler. Besides waging wars with Iran and Kuwait, Saddam also used his armed might against his own people, especially the minority Kurds in the north.

Saddam Hussein was born on April 28, 1937, to a peasant family in Tikrit, a village in northern Iraq. Orphaned early in life, he was raised for a time by an uncle. After moving to Baghdad to attend secondary school, he joined the Ba'th party in 1957, and in 1959 he participated in an unsuccessful plot to assassinate 'Abd al-Karim Qasim, the Iraqi prime minister. After the failed coup Saddam fled Iraq, going first to Syria and then to Egypt. In Cairo he came under the powerful influence of Egyptian President Gamal Abdel Nasser, whom Saddam had admired since Nasser's own successful rise to power in 1952.

With Nasser's help, Saddam enrolled at Cairo Law School in 1962 but returned to Baghdad the following year after Qasim was deposed. Saddam joined the Ba'ath Party's new government. The new regime was short-lived, however and Saddam was arrested and imprisoned.He escaped from confinement in 1966 and soon was elected to a prominent position in the Ba'ath Party.

In 1968 the Ba'ath Party seized control of the Iraqi government in a bloodless coup and installed party head Ahmad Hassan al-Bakr as president and head of the Revolutionary Command Council, or RCC. Bakr, a relative of Saddam's, worked closely with the latter to dominate Ba'athist policies. As deputy chairman of the RCC, Saddam soon became the most powerful and feared individual in government. He worked relentlessly to get rid of opponents and place friends and family in positions of authority.

To revitalize the flagging Iraqi economy, Saddam in 1972 ordered the nationalization of Iraq's oil industry. Revenues poured in and the high oil revenues also enabled Iraq to build its military.

During the 1970s Saddam continued to gain power. In 1979 he assumed the presidency after convincing the ailing Bakr to resign. Once in office, Saddam quickly ordered the execution of 22 high-ranking political rivals. He also established a secret police force to suppress political and popular opposition to his rule.

Relations between Iran and Iraq began deteriorating in the 1970s. Among other incidents, Iran had backed a rebellion staged in 1974 by Kurds living in northern Iraq, a revolt brutally and quickly suppressed by Saddam's regime. Following a series of border skirmishes with Iran in 1980, Iraq launched a full-scale invasion of Iran's oil fields, a war that lasted eight years.

During the Iran-Iraq War, Iraq used chemical weapons on Iranian troops as well as Iraqi Kurdish guerrilla fighters, who had joined the

Iranian offensive. Also, in the late 1980s chemical agents were used against Kurdish communities in northern Iraq. Thousands of civilians were killed, and many more sustained permanent health problems.

By the late 1980s Iraq had accrued an enormous foreign debt from the cost of the Iran-Iraq War and its necessary interruption of oil exports. Despite this burden, Saddam continued to expand the military. In August 1990 Iraq invaded neighboring Kuwait. The United Nations (UN) condemned the occupation and authorized a military intervention to end it if necessary. In January 1991 a U.S.-led military coalition moved into the region; six weeks later, coalition forces had liberated Kuwait.

Over the next decade, Saddam's refusal to cooperate with UN weapons inspectors brought worldwide economic sanctions and periodic air strikes by the United States and Great Britain. Impatient and wary over Saddam's lack of compliance, the United States and Great Britain in early 2003 warned Saddam of swift military action if disarmament was not completed promptly. In March 2003, U.S. President George W. Bush ordered Saddam to leave the country or face removal by force. Saddam refused to leave, and on March 20, 2003, a U.S.- and British-led coalition invaded Iraq. Saddam, along with his family and closest advisers, immediately went into hiding. Within months of the invasion a number of Saddam's advisers were found by advancing coalition forces, and in July 2003, two of Saddam's sons were killed during a raid of their hideout by U.S. troops. Saddam eluded capture until Dec. 13, 2003, when U.S. troops discovered the former dictator in an underground hideout near his hometown of Tikrit. Although armed, Saddam surrendered without a struggle and was taken into custody.

In October 2005 Saddam went on trial before the Iraqi High Tribunal, a panel court established to try officials of the former Iraqi government. The tribunal adjourned in July 2006 and handed down its verdicts in November. Saddam was convicted of crimes against humanity, including willful killing, illegal imprisonment, deportation, and torture, and sentenced to death by hanging. Saddam's half brother (an intelligence officer) and Iraq's former chief judge also were sentenced to death. Days after an Iraqi court upheld his sentence, Saddam was hanged in Baghdad on Dec. 30, 2006.

SALADIN

(b. 1137/38–d. 1193)

During the First Crusade Christian warriors from Europe captured most of Palestine and its chief city, Jerusalem. After holding the city for 88 years, it was taken from them on Oct. 2, 1187, by the armies of Saladin, the most famous of Muslim military heroes.

Saladin was born in 1137 or 1138 in Takrit, Mesopotamia. He grew up in Aleppo, Ba'lbek, and Damascus. As a teenager he showed more inclination to become a Muslim scholar than a soldier. His military career began when he joined the staff of his uncle, Asad ad-Din Shirkuh, a commander under the governor of northern Syria. When his uncle died, Saladin—at age 31—was appointed commander of the troops and vizier of Egypt. In 1171 he abolished the Fatimid Caliphate of Egypt and became the country's sole ruler. From 1174 to 1186 Saladin pursued the goal of uniting Egypt, Syria, Palestine, and northern Mesopotamia under his flag. He accomplished this mostly by diplomacy, but he used force when necessary. He turned the military balance in his favor by 1187 and threw his armies against the Christian knights. He destroyed one of their armies near Tiberias and then went on to conquer Acre, Toron, Beirut, Sidon, Nazareth, Caesarea, Nabulus, Jaffa, and Ascalon. Finally he captured Jerusalem. Saladin's conquest was civilized and magnanimous.

The Christians were left with the well-fortified city of Tyre as their last major outpost in the Middle East. Saladin's achievement spurred Europe to launch the Third Crusade, which failed to undo Saladin's conquests. After defeating the last of the new crusaders in October 1192, Saladin returned to Damascus. He died there on March 4, 1193.

SHIHUANGDI

(b. 259 BCE–d. 210 BCE)

Shihuangdi, Wade-Giles Shih-huang-ti, personal name (*xingming*) Zhao Zheng or Ying Zheng. He was emperor (reigned 221–210 BCE) of the Qin dynasty (221–207 BCE) and creator of the first unified Chinese empire (which collapsed, however, less than four years after his death).

Zhao Zheng was born on 259 BCE in Qin state in northwestern China. He was the son of Zhuangxiang (who later became king of the state of Qin in northwestern China) and was born while his father was held hostage in the state of Zhao. His mother was a former concubine of a rich merchant, Lü Buwei. Buwei, guided by financial interests, managed to install Zhuangxiang on the throne, even though he had not originally been designated as successor.

When Zheng, at age 13, formally came to the throne in 246 BCE, Qin already was the most powerful state and was likely to unite the rest of China under its rule. He succeeded in completing the conquests, and in 221 BCE he created the Qin dynasty. To announce his achievement, Zheng assumed the sacred titles of legendary rulers and proclaimed himself Shihuangdi ("First Sovereign Emperor").

Until Zheng was officially declared of age in 238, his government was headed by Lü Buwei. Zheng's first act as king was to either exile or execute his mother's lover, who had joined the opposition. By 221, with the help of espionage, extensive bribery, and the ruthlessly effective leadership of gifted generals, Zheng had eliminated one by one the remaining six rival states that constituted China at that time. He united China was united, under the supreme rule of the Qin.

With unbounded confidence, he claimed that his dynasty would last "10,000 generations." As emperor he initiated a series of reforms aimed at establishing a fully centralized administration, thus avoiding the rise of independent satrapies. He divided the country into 36 military districts, each with its own military and civil administrator. Construction of a network of roads and canals was begun, and fortresses erected for defense against barbarian invasions from the north were linked to form the Great Wall. He standardized the Chinese writing system and had the Great Wall of China built.

The continuous controversy between the emperor and Confucian scholars who advocated a return to the old feudal order culminated in the famous burning of the books of 213, when, at Li Si's suggestion, all books not dealing with agriculture, medicine, or prognostication were burned, except historical records of Qin and books in the imperial library.

The last years of Shihuangdi's life were dominated by an ever-growing distrust of his entourage—at least three assassination attempts nearly succeeded—and his increasing isolation from the common people. Almost inaccessible in his huge palaces, the emperor led the life of a semi-divine being. In 210 Shihuangdi died during an inspection tour in Heiwei. He was buried in a gigantic funerary compound hewn out of a mountain and shaped in conformity with the symbolic patterns of the cosmos. The disappearance of Shihuangdi's forceful personality immediately led to the outbreak of fighting among supporters of the old feudal factions that ended in the collapse of the Qin dynasty and the extermination of the entire imperial clan by 206.

Most of the information about Shihuangdi's life derives from the successor Han dynasty, which prized Confucian scholarship and thus had an interest in disparaging the Qin period. The report that Shihuangdi was an illegitimate son of Lü Buwei is possibly an invention of that epoch.

Shihuangdi certainly had an imposing personality and showed an unbending will in pursuing his aim of uniting and strengthening the empire. With few exceptions, the traditional chronicles of imperial China have regarded him as the villain, inhuman, uncultivated, and superstitious. Modern historians, however, generally stress the endurance of the bureaucratic and administrative structure set up by Shihuangdi, which, despite its official denial, remained the basis of all subsequent dynasties in China.

SITTING BULL

(b. 1831?–d. 1890)

The Hunkpapa Sioux Indian chief and medicine man Sitting Bull was respected by the Native Americans of the Plains for his courage and wisdom and feared by settlers and the United States Army for his determination to rid Indian tribal lands of white people. Under him the Sioux tribes united in their struggle for survival on the Great Plains.

Sitting Bull was born in about 1831 near Grand River in the Dakota Territory. The Hunkpapa Sioux were a nomadic and warlike tribe, and Sitting Bull had his first skirmish with white soldiers in June 1863. For the next five years he frequently fought the army. He was made principal chief of the Sioux nation in about 1867. When gold was discovered in the Black Hills in the mid-1870s, a rush of prospectors invaded the Indian lands.

In late 1875 all Sioux were ordered to move to reservations. Sitting Bull refused to go, and the army was mobilized to remove him and his people. Sitting Bull summoned the Sioux, Cheyenne, and certain Arapaho to his camp in the Little Bighorn River valley.

Photographic portrait of Sioux Indian Chief Sitting Bull. Library of Congress Prints and Photographs Division

He foretold that soldiers would fall into his camp like grasshoppers from the sky. His prophecy was fulfilled on June 25, 1876, when Lieut. Col. George Armstrong Custer and his soldiers rode into the valley and were annihilated.

Sitting Bull led his people to Canada, where they depended on the buffalo for their livelihood. When there were no more buffalo to hunt, they were forced to surrender in 1881. In 1885 he was allowed to join Buffalo Bill's Wild West Show. Sitting Bull was killed on December 15, 1890, on the Grand River in South Dakota as his warriors were trying to prevent his arrest.

JOSEPH STALIN

(b. 1879–d. 1953)

One of the most ruthless dictators of modern times was Joseph Stalin, the despot who transformed the Soviet Union into a major world power. The victims of his campaigns of political terror included some of his followers. His real name was Iosif Vissarionovich Dzhugashvili. In 1912 he took the alias of "Stalin," from the Russian word *stal*, meaning "steel."

Joseph Stalin was born in Gori, a village in Transcaucasian Georgia, on Dec. 18, 1879. His father was Vissarion Dzhugashvili, a poor shoemaker who drank heavily and beat the boy savagely. His mother, a peasant's daughter, took in sewing and washing to help support the family.

Stalin entered a church school at the age of nine. At 14 his father died, and the boy was sent to be educated for the priesthood. He was more interested in Communism, however, than in theology, and the seminary expelled him in 1899 as an agitator. He soon joined the Tiflis branch of the Russian Social Democratic Party.

Stalin then became a paid agitator, trying to incite revolt against the czar. He organized strikes among the factory workers in Tiflis. His ability won the attention of party leaders, and they sent him to form a Communist organization in Batumi, a large port on the Black Sea.

His revolutionist activities brought his first arrest, in 1902. He was exiled to Siberia in 1903 but soon escaped. Like his fellow revolutionaries, he adopted one alias after another in order to evade arrest. Stalin was also one of his aliases.

In 1903 the Social Democratic Party split into two factions. One faction, headed by Lenin, called itself the Bolsheviks. Stalin believed in Lenin's policy, and so he joined the Bolsheviks.

His iron zeal and organizing ability won Lenin's high regard. Shrewd Lenin worked with Stalin closely. In 1912 Lenin made him a member of the Central Committee. Meanwhile Stalin wrote for the Bolshevik newspaper *Pravda* ("Truth"), which he is said to have founded. Arrested again, in 1912, he again escaped within a few months.

He helped Lenin prepare the final plans for the history-making Bolshevik revolution. Stalin's name seldom appears in records of the revolution, for he remained in the background as an administrator. His work was largely responsible for the success of the bloody October Revolution, in 1917.

During the civil war that followed the revolution Stalin showed exceptional ability as a strategist and tactician. In 1918 he directed the successful defense of vital Tsaritsyn against the White Army. The city was renamed Stalingrad in his honor in 1925, though the name was later changed to Volgograd as part of an effort in the 1950s and 1960s to downgrade Stalin's importance. In 1922 Stalin became general secretary of the Central Committee of the Communist Party, as the Bolsheviks now called themselves. As Lenin's trusted aide, Stalin methodically assumed increasing power.

Some of Stalin's unscrupulous methods worried even Lenin. Stalin, however, was undisturbed by criticism. Grimly he undermined his rival Leon Trotsky, the Soviet Union's war minister and Lenin's former close associate. Stalin expelled him from the party in 1927. Determined to eliminate the minority Trotskyite influence, Stalin exiled Trotsky from the Soviet Union in 1929 and had him assassinated in 1940.

Having dealt with the opposition Stalin was then supreme ruler. In a drive to industrialize and modernize the Soviet Union, he launched the first in a series of five-year plans in 1928.

Stalin ordered the collectivization of farms. When peasants resisted, he ordered the state to seize their land and possessions. Well-to-do farmers, called *kulaks*, especially resented collectivization. In 1932–33 he created a famine in Ukraine and liquidated some 3 million *kulaks* through death by starvation.

In 1936 Stalin's ruthless methods again drew world attention. To consolidate his place as supreme dictator, he conducted a series of purges. In August 1939 Stalin startled the world again when he brought the Soviet Union into a nonaggression pact with Nazi Germany just before World War II. The nonaggression pact permitted the Soviets to seize eastern Poland, attack Finland, and absorb the Romanian provinces of Bessarabia and Bukovina without German opposition. Stalin extended Soviet borders into outlying buffer areas.

In May 1941 Stalin made himself premier. In June the Soviet Union was invaded by Germany. Stalin took command of the army and reorganized industry. After the war's end, Stalin seemed to be determined to make the Soviet Union dominant in Europe and to impose Communism on the world. Through purges and other relentless measures he forced Communist governments on Eastern Europe and sought to gain control of Italy and France. In the United Nations and in Allied councils, his obstructionist policy blocked efforts to establish a lasting peace. His blockade of Berlin in 1948–49 threatened a third global war.

Many of the dates and facts of Stalin's personal life remain uncertain. He was married in 1903, at the age of 24, to Ekaterina Svanidze, a native of Georgia. She died in 1907 of tuberculosis. Their son, Yasha, died in a Nazi prison camp during World War II. In 1919 Stalin married Nadya Alliluyeva, who died in 1932. They had a daughter, Svetlana, and a son, Vassili, a Soviet air force officer. Vassili died in 1962. In 1967 Svetlana, who used her mother's maiden name, defected to the United States.

Stalin died on March 5, 1953. Four days after his death, his embalmed body was entombed alongside that of Lenin in Moscow's Red Square. In February 1956 Nikita Khrushchev, then first secretary of the Soviet Communist Party, addressed the 20th Soviet Communist Party Congress in secret session. He devoted three hours to the systematic destruction of Joseph Stalin's image as a public hero.

Among other charges, Stalin was accused of wanton slaughter during the prewar purge trials, of being abnormally suspicious of associates, and of causing thousands of unnecessary casualties during World War II by incompetently interfering with Red Army campaigns. Above all he was denounced for having paraded himself as a savior.

SUKARNO

(b. 1901–d. 1970)

The leader of the Indonesian independence movement and the first president of his country was Sukarno. (Single names are quite common in Indonesia.) As president he headed a mismanaged and corrupt administration that virtually destroyed the government and economy of Indonesia. Yet his magnetic personality and oratorical skills held the loyalty of the masses almost until he was overthrown by Suharto in 1966 after an attempted Communist revolt.

Sukarno was born on June 6, 1901, in Surabaja, Java, in the Dutch East Indies. He grew up there and with his grandparents in Tulungagung. After high school in Surabaja he attended the Bandung Technical Institute, graduating in 1925. He had a degree in civil engineering but soon found politics far more appealing. His eloquent speaking ability soon made him Java's foremost proponent of independence. He was jailed (1929–31) and exiled (1933–42) for his views.

When the Japanese invaded Java in 1942, he welcomed them as liberators and cooperated with them. At the end of World War II, Sukarno declared his country independent as Indonesia. The Dutch gave up trying to regain the islands in 1949. Sukarno then installed himself in the capital city, Jakarta, where he lived in extravagant luxury. In 1956 he dismantled the constitutional government and began the destruction of free enterprise.

In 1965, still popular with the people, he was implicated in the murder of six army officers by Communist conspirators. The commander of the Jakarta garrison, General Suharto, put down a Communist insurrection. The public demanded an end to Sukarno's rule. On March 11, 1966, he was forced to delegate most of his powers to Suharto. By March 1968 he was out of office, ill, and somewhat senile. He died of a long-time kidney ailment on June 21, 1970, in Jakarta.

SUN YAT-SEN

(b. 1866–d. 1925)

Known as the father of modern China, Sun Yat-sen worked to achieve his lofty goals to transform the country. These included the successful overthrow of the Qing, or Manchu, dynasty and the establishment of a republic. He was the first provisional president of the Republic of China in 1911–12 and leader of the Chinese Nationalist Party, or Kuomintang. He came to power again in 1923–25. His name is also spelled (in Pinyin) Sun Yixian.

Sun Yat-sen was born on Nov. 12, 1866, in Xiangshan (now Zhongshan), Guangdong Province, China. He attended several schools, including ones in Honolulu, Hawaii, before transferring to a college of medicine in Hong Kong. During this period, he converted to Christianity. Graduating in 1892, Sun almost immediately abandoned medicine for politics. China had clung to its traditional ways under the conservative Manchu government. Sun wanted China to modernize and become stronger so that it could better protect itself against ongoing aggression by foreign countries.

In 1894 Sun founded an anti-Manchu society, which was the forerunner of several secret revolutionary groups that he would later lead. His role in plotting an unsuccessful uprising in Guangzhou (Canton) in 1895 prompted him to begin an exile that lasted for 16 years. Sun used this time to travel widely in Japan, Europe, and the United States, enlisting sympathy and raising money for his cause.

While abroad, he planned several revolts, but they all failed. Sun returned to China in 1911 after a rebellion in Wuhan overthrew the government of Hubei Province and inspired successful uprisings in several other provinces. Sun was elected provisional president of the newly declared republic. Sun knew that his regime was weak, so he made a deal with a powerful imperial minister, Yuan Shikai. Yuan successfully convinced the Manchu emperor to step down in early 1912, and Sun resigned so that Yuan could become president of the republic.

Yuan did not govern democratically, however, and plotted to have several of his opponents killed. In 1913 Sun organized a second revolution, to overthrow Yuan. Failing to regain power, Sun left once again for Japan. After Yuan's death in 1916, warlords took over many parts of the country. Sun returned to China and attempted to set up a new government in 1917 and 1921 before successfully installing himself as generalissimo of a new Nationalist Party regime in southern China in 1923.

Sun increasingly relied on aid from the Soviet Union, and in 1924 he reorganized the Nationalist Party on the model of the Soviet Communist party. Sun also founded the Whampoa Military Academy and appointed Chiang Kai-shek as its president. Sun summarized his policies in the Three Principles of the People—nationalism, democracy, and socialism.

He died in Beijing on March 12, 1925. Sun's tomb in Nanjing is now a national shrine.

MARGARET THATCHER

(b. 1925–d. 2013)

The first woman to be elected prime minister of the United Kingdom, Margaret Thatcher was also the first woman to hold such a post in the history of Europe. The first prime minister since the 1820s to win three consecutive elections, Thatcher held office longer than any other 20th-century British leader.

Margaret Hilda Roberts was born on October 13, 1925, at Grantham, Lincolnshire, England. She ran errands for the Conservative Party in the 1935 election and maintained this association as a member of the Oxford University Conservative Association. A science graduate of Oxford, she worked as a research chemist.

Her first attempts to win a seat in Parliament were in 1950 and 1951. She lost both elections. In 1951 she married businessman Denis Thatcher. To equip herself for politics she began studying law, with an emphasis on taxation and patent policy. In 1959 Thatcher ran again

Margaret Thatcher, celebrating her election as British prime minister in 1983. Peter Jordan/Time & Life Pictures/Getty Images

for Parliament from a safe Conservative north London district and won. She served as secretary to the Ministry of Pensions and Insurance from 1961 to 1964 and as secretary of state for education and science in Edward Heath's Cabinet from 1970 to 1974. After the Conservative Party's loss of two general elections in 1974, she followed Heath as head of the party. When the Conservative Party won the 1979 elections, Thatcher became prime minister.

She belonged to the most conservative wing of her party, advocating cuts in taxation, an end to government controls, and reductions in public expenditures. Her early policies caused widespread unemployment and a number of business bankruptcies. A popular victory in the Falkland Islands conflict of 1982, however, led to a landslide victory in the 1983 elections. Her stature as a world leader increased when she visited the Soviet Union in March 1987, less than three months before she won another remarkable victory.

Thatcher's declared objective was to "destroy socialism." Her "unfinished revolution" to reshape British political, economic, and social life—mainly through privatization—was labeled Thatcherism. Because of her strong leadership, she was called the Iron Lady. She supported the NATO alliance and the European Communities, though her opposition to "Europe 1992" integration adversely affected her popularity and helped lead to her resignation in November 1990.

Despite her official withdrawal from office, Thatcher continued to cast a shadow over world politics. She was especially outspoken in her opposition to Britain's participation in several institutions of the European Union, and she outlined her position in her book *Statecraft: Strategies for a Changing World* (2002). In 1991 she established the Margaret Thatcher Foundation, which promotes democracy and free markets, particularly in the formerly Communist countries of Eastern and Central Europe. She was made a peeress for life in the House of Lords in 1992, and in 1995 Queen Elizabeth II conferred upon her the Order of the Garter, the highest British civil and military honor.

In March 2002, after suffering a series of minor strokes, Thatcher announced her retirement from public life. She died on April 8, 2013, in London, England.

TITO

(b. 1892–d. 1980)

The Yugoslav Partisans, an army of freedom fighters who successfully fought Hitler's armies in World War II, were led by Tito. After the war he became the leader of the new Yugoslav socialist state. Officially elected president on Jan. 13, 1953, Tito remained the ruler of Yugoslavia until his death.

By breaking with the Soviet leader Joseph Stalin, he proclaimed the right of each socialist nation to pursue its own course. He also conducted and promoted a policy of not politically committing his country to support either the Soviet Union or the United States. This led to close ties with other neutralist leaders, such as Egypt's President Gamal Abdel Nasser and India's Prime Minister Jawaharlal Nehru, and the founding of a conference of nonaligned countries in 1961. With them he denounced colonialism and proclaimed the equality of large and small states.

Josip Broz was born on May 7, 1892, at Kumrovec, on the border of Croatia and Slovenia. He began to call himself Tito in 1934, when he was often being prosecuted for his political activities. He had little formal education. By age 13 he was learning to be a locksmith, and later worked as a metalworker. He fought in World War I, was seriously wounded, and was captured by the Russian Army.

He returned from Russia in 1920, and it was during the next few years that he became active in the Communist Party of Yugoslavia (CPY). For his political activities he was arrested several times. The longest imprisonment was from 1928 to 1934. By 1940 Tito was general secretary of the CPY.

After Germany attacked Yugoslavia on April 6, 1941, Tito became the leader of Partisan resistance. The resistance spread throughout the country, and over the next several years the Partisans fought heavy battles against the Germans but were undefeated. In 1943 Tito was given the title of marshal of Yugoslavia, and he was normally referred to as Marshal Tito from that time.

161

After the war Tito established a Communist government in Yugoslavia. By this he alienated the United States and other Western nations, which were also opposed to his support for Communist insurgents in Greece and his attempt to seize the Italian city of Trieste. While his relations with the West deteriorated, he also made an enemy of Stalin by his determination to preserve Yugoslav independence. Stalin broke with Tito by expelling the CPY from the Communist Information Bureau on June 28, 1948.

After Stalin's death in 1953, the new Soviet leaders accepted Tito's independent course. Tito made the administration of Yugoslav government less centralized. He established workers' councils in factories and granted greater freedoms to the citizens than were allowed in other Communist countries at the time. He also pursued his policy of nonalignment with either the United States or the Soviet Union. In 1970 he announced a plan for a collective presidency, by which Yugoslavia came to be governed after his death on May 4, 1980, at Ljubljana.

PIERRE ELLIOTT TRUDEAU

(b. 1919–d. 2000)

Within three years after he first held public office, Pierre Elliott Trudeau was the head of the Canadian government. In April 1968 the bilingual Liberal Party leader became Canada's 15th prime minister.

Joseph Philippe Pierre Ives Elliott Trudeau was born in Montreal, Que., on Oct. 18, 1919, the second of three children. A graduate of Collège Jean-de-Brébeuf and the University of Montreal Law School, Trudeau studied political economy at Harvard University, the University of Paris, and the London School of Economics. He also traveled extensively.

In 1950 Trudeau founded a social-reform magazine called *Free City* that opposed the Union Nationale regime in Quebec. He wrote several books, including *Two Innocents in Red China* (published in 1961) and *Federalism and the French Canadians* (1968).

In 1952 Trudeau opened a labor-law practice in Montreal. He joined the law faculty of the University of Montreal in 1960. Five years later he was elected to the House of Commons as a "new wave" Liberal. Trudeau was made parliamentary secretary to Prime Minister Lester B. Pearson in 1966 and in 1967 was appointed the minister of justice and attorney general. As minister of justice, Trudeau was successful in passing measures for stricter gun control and the reform of laws against abortion and homosexuality.

An opponent of Quebec separatism, Trudeau gained the Liberal Party leadership on pledges of a "united Canada" and a "free and just society." He became the third French Canadian prime minister in April 1968, after Pearson retired.

Trudeau's popularity—particularly with younger voters—was demonstrated when he won a parliamentary majority in the June 1968 general election. He introduced legislation to streamline the government and to promote bilingualism. His government remained in office after an election in October 1972 that was the closest in Canadian history. Although it fell in May 1974 on the issue of rising inflation, Trudeau regained unchallenged control of Parliament in the July election. Throughout the 1970s, however, he was criticized for the country's increasing economic and domestic problems. The Liberals lost in May 1979, and Joe Clark, leader of the Progressive Conservatives, formed a new government.

In the election of February 1980, in a stunning political comeback, Trudeau gained his fourth term as prime minister. He achieved his longtime plan to reform Canada's constitution. Under his leadership, Canada became a fully sovereign state in 1982. Trudeau spent his next two years in office concentrating on gaining greater economic independence for Canada, seeking more international disarmament talks, and improving trade relations with other countries, especially Third World nations. Trudeau announced his decision to retire in early 1984 and officially resigned on June 30 after a new party leader was chosen. Trudeau died on Sept. 28, 2000, in Montreal.

VICTORIA

(b. 1819–d. 1901)

On June 22, 1897, as cheering throngs massed in the streets, cannon roared, and the bells of London rang, a carriage pulled up to the

Photographic portrait of Queen Victoria. Keystone-France/Gamma-Keystone/ Getty Images

steps of St. Paul's Cathedral. The greatest empire on Earth was paying tribute to Victoria, the queen-empress, on her Diamond Jubilee.

Alexandrina Victoria of the House of Hanover was born at Kensington Palace in London on May 24, 1819. Her father, the Duke of Kent, was the fourth son of George III. Her mother was a German princess.

Victoria was 18 years old when she became queen of the United Kingdom upon the death of her uncle William IV in 1837. She was crowned at Westminster Abbey on June 28, 1838.

The young Victoria met and fell in love with her first cousin Prince Albert of Saxe-Coburg-Gotha. They were married in 1840 after Victoria had decided that as queen it was her right to propose to Albert. It was a happy marriage. Albert's political life, however, was difficult. The queen had insisted that he be given the title of prince consort. But the government and many of the people were critical. They objected to any part the prince took in advising the queen on affairs of state.

Victoria and Albert had nine children. She arranged their marriages. Her eldest daughter became empress of Germany and mother of William II, and her granddaughter was the last empress of Russia. By the end of the 19th century, Victoria had so many royal relatives that she was called the "grandmother of Europe."

After Albert's untimely death in 1861, Victoria went into seclusion. She avoided London and spent most of her time at Balmoral Castle in Scotland, at Osborne House on the Isle of Wight, and at Windsor.

In 1875 Britain gained control of the Suez Canal, and Victoria was proclaimed empress of India in 1876. Disraeli's fall from power in 1880 was a blow to the queen. The "widow of Windsor," in a long self-imposed isolation, became an almost legendary figure until the last years of her reign. The longest reign in British history (64 years), it was marked with the glitter and pageantry of her Golden Jubilee in 1887 and her Diamond Jubilee in 1897.

Victoria was not a great ruler or a particularly brilliant woman. She was fortunate through most of her reign in having a succession of politically able Cabinet ministers. She happened, however, to be queen of Great Britain for most of the 19th century—a century that saw more changes than any previous period in history. The queen became the living symbol of peace and prosperity.

Victoria had lived from the dissolute days of George III to the beginning of the 20th century. She made the Crown a symbol of "private virtue and public honor." Victoria died on the Isle of Wight on Jan. 22, 1901.

LECH WAŁĘSA

(b. 1943–)

Solidarity, Poland's first independent trade union under a Communist regime, was founded by Lech Wałęsa in 1980. He gained recognition around the world as the leader of millions of Poland's workers. In an attempt to crush the union, the government imposed martial law on Dec. 13, 1981, an act that only enhanced Wałęsa's reputation. He was awarded the Nobel Peace Prize in 1983.

Wałęsa was born in Popowo, Poland, on Sept. 29, 1943. His father was a carpenter, and young Wałęsa received only elementary schooling followed by vocational training. In 1967 he went to work as an electrician at the Lenin Shipyard in Gdańsk. In 1970 there were worker riots against higher food prices. Many of the demonstrators were gunned down by government troops.

On Aug. 14, 1980, during more antigovernment protests, Wałęsa urged the workers to strike. When strikers in other factories asked him to continue the strike in solidarity with them, he agreed. An inter-factory strike committee was formed and a general strike proclaimed. On August 31 the government agreed to permit the formation of inde-pendent unions. The strike committee was transformed into Solidarity. After the government imposed martial law in 1981, Solidarity was outlawed and most of its leaders arrested. Wałęsa was detained for nearly a year.

It was the re-legalization of Solidarity as a trade union in April 1989 and the agreement to hold partially free parliamentary elections that appeared to open the door for the radical reforms that influenced other countries of the Soviet bloc in their effort to challenge the Communist system. Solidarity candidates scored a stunning victory in June elections, and in August a prominent member became premier—the first instance of a non-Communist being chosen head of a Communist nation in Eastern Europe.

In November Wałęsa visited the United States, where he addressed a joint session of Congress. A split in Solidarity was prompted by Wałęsa's criticism of the government. In December 1990 he was elected presi-dent of Poland, succeeding Gen. Wojciech Jaruzelski. After serving one term, he was defeated by ex-Communist Aleksander Kwasniewski in the November 1995 presidential election.

GEORGE WASHINGTON

(b. 1732–d. 1799)

United States President George Washington's achievements distin-guished him as the Father of His Country. Washington was the first president of the United States. He led the people who transformed the United States from a British colony into a self-governing nation. His ideals of liberty and democracy set a standard for future presidents and for the entire country.

George Washington was born on February 22 (February 11 on the calendar used then), 1732, on the Wakefield plantation in Westmoreland County, Virginia. Washington heard many stories of his brother's experi-ences in the British navy. These tales inspired Washington to pursue a military career. In 1753 he was made a major of an army militia, and his skill led him to be lieutenant colonel by April 1754. His attack on a French scouting party contributed to the start of the French and Indian War.

Washington's skillful maneuvers in the ambush against the French scouting party were recognized by his superior officers, and he was immediately promoted to colonel. In August 1755 he became commander of all Virginia militia forces. In 1758 Washington accompanied British Gen. John Forbes and finally defeated the French at Fort Duquesne. Washington resigned from

Portrait of George Washington, by Charles Wilson Peale. Culture Club/Hulton Archive/ Getty Images

the army with the honorary rank of brigadier general. While serving in the final campaign against Fort Duquesne, Washington was elected to the Virginia House of Burgesses.

Great Britain continued to regulate the colonies in matters of taxation and legislation with the Townshend Acts of 1767, which placed taxes on imported British commodities. In April 1769 Washington presented a plan to the House of Burgesses for boycotting British-made goods. On December 16, 1773, a group of colonists threw 342 chests of tea into Boston Harbor to protest a tea tax. This rebellion was known as the Boston Tea Party.

Washington's political career expanded as dissension grew between the colonists and Great Britain. He believed that the British had attacked the rights of the colonists with heavy taxes and oppressive laws, and he was ready to defend these rights. In May 1774 Washington and other Virginia legislators signed the resolutions calling for a Continental Congress. He was elected to the Virginia delegation that attended the First Continental Congress in Philadelphia on September 5, 1774.

Recognizing Washington's military experience and leadership, the Continental Congress made him commander in chief of all colonial military forces in June 1775. Washington commanded the respect of his troops through his confidence, poise, and determination as a general. In March 1776 his army staged a siege and eventually expelled British troops from Boston.

On July 4, 1776, the Continental Congress adopted the Declaration of Independence for the 13 colonies. Congress wrote the Articles of Confederation, the first constitution in the United States, to implement a national government.

By 1778 France recognized the United States as an independent nation and sent military support to help Washington's forces fight the British. After further battles, the Treaty of Paris was signed on September 3, 1783, officially ending the American Revolution.

On February 4, 1789, the electors granted all 69 electoral votes to George Washington, thereby unanimously electing him as president of the United States. John Adams was elected vice president. Washington was inaugurated into office on April 30, 1789. His presidency was to be a time of adjustment to a new type of government for the people of the United States.

During Washington's administration, the authority of the federal government was greatly strengthened. Washington and Alexander Hamilton chartered the Bank of the United States in 1791. In 1791 the states ratified the Bill of Rights, the first 10 amendments to the Constitution, which granted United States citizens their basic rights. Washington was reelected to a second term as president in 1792, with John Adams again serving as his vice president.

When war broke out between France and Great Britain in 1793, Washington decided that the United States should remain neutral in foreign affairs. Accordingly, he issued the Proclamation of Neutrality in April 1793, which stated that the United States must maintain a sense of national identity, independent from any other country's influence.

When Washington's second term ended in 1796, he refused to run for a third term. He considered it unwise for one person to hold such a powerful position for so long. Washington retired to Mount Vernon where he died on December 14, 1799. He was buried in the family vault at Mount Vernon.

In 1800 the United States capital was moved from Philadelphia to the newly developed city of Washington, D.C., named in honor of George Washington. In 1853 Congress created the Washington Territory, which became a state in 1889, and named it in memory of the nation's first president. The Washington Monument, in Washington, D.C., is yet another lasting tribute to the man considered by most Americans to be the Father of His Country.

WILLIAM I

(b. 1028?–d. 1087)

In 1066 William, duke of Normandy, invaded England, defeated the king, and seized the English crown. As king he took the title William I, but he is commonly called William the Conqueror. The Norman Conquest changed the course of English history.

William was born about 1028 in Falaise, Normandy (now in France). He was an illegitimate son of Robert I, duke of Normandy. His mother was a tanner's daughter. When Robert died in 1035, William succeeded him as duke. By his early 20s, William had made himself the mightiest feudal lord in all France by various conquests, but his ambition was not satisfied. He also laid plans to become king of England.

William married Matilda, daughter of Baldwin V, count of Flanders, in 1053. Among their children were four sons including Robert, future duke of Normandy; William Rufus, who succeeded his father as king of England; and Henry, who succeeded William Rufus. One daughter, Adela, became the mother of England's King Stephen.

William was a cousin of Edward the Confessor, king of England. He used his connection with Flanders to put pressure on Edward to extort a promise that he would become heir to the English throne. Edward died childless on January 5, 1066. William then claimed the throne on the basis of this promise. The English, however, chose Harold Godwinson, Earl of Wessex, as their king. He was crowned as Harold II.

William prepared a large expedition and set sail for England. On October 14, 1066, he defeated and killed Harold at Hastings in one of the decisive battles of the world. Then he marched on London, and on Christmas Day he was crowned king.

After subduing England's powerful earls, William seized their lands and distributed them among his elite Norman followers. These men, numbering fewer than 180, became the nobility of Norman England. William ordered the nobles to build fortified stone castles to protect their lands. As payment for their lands, the nobles supplied the king with armed knights. Soon the nobles began to grant some of their lands to knights who would serve them just as they in turn served the king. This exchange of land for military service, known as feudalism, had originated in Normandy. The Normans also introduced French as the language of the king's court; it gradually blended with the Anglo-Saxon tongue.

William won the loyalty of the mass of the people by wisely retaining the old Anglo-Saxon laws, courts, and customs with only a few changes. Thus the principle of self-government, which lies at the root of the political system of English-speaking peoples, was preserved and strengthened. At the same time, William taught the English the advantages of a central government strong enough to control feudal lords.

William was often on the Continent dealing with his widespread holdings. He died in Rouen, Normandy (now in France), on September 9, 1087, from injuries received while warring with the French king Philip I.

GLOSSARY

ABOLITIONIST A person who favors the abolition of a practice or institution, especially capital punishment or (formerly) slavery.

AMNESTY The act of an authority (as a government) by which pardon is granted to a large group of individuals.

BUREAUCRACY A body of nonelected government officials; an administrative group.

CIVILIAN One who is not on active duty in the armed forces.

CIVIL WAR A war between citizens of the same country.

COMMUNISM A theory or system of social organization in which all property is owned by the community and each person contributes and receives according to their ability and needs.

COUP A sudden, violent, and illegal seizure of power from a government.

FASCISM An authoritarian and nationalistic system of government and social organization.

GENOCIDE The deliberate and systematic destruction of a racial, political, or cultural group.

GUERRILLA A person who engages in irregular warfare especially as a member of an independent unit carrying out sabotage and harassment.

INSURGENT A person who revolts against civil authority or an established government.

JUNTA A military or political group that rules a country after taking power by force.

PERESTROIKA In Russian society, the policy or practice of restructuring or reforming the economic and political system.

QUAESTOR One of numerous Roman officials concerned chiefly with financial administration.

REGENT A person who governs a kingdom in the minority, absence, or disability of the sovereign.

REGIME A mode of rule or government; a period of rule

SEGREGATE Separate or divide along racial, sexual, or religious lines.

SOCIALISM A political and economic theory of social organization that advocates that the means of production, distribution, and exchange should be owned or regulated by the community as a whole.

WELFARE A uniform procedure or social effort designed to promote the basic physical and material well-being of people in need.

Institute of Political Leadership
P.O. Box 8009
Greensboro, NC 27419
(336) 333-9010
Web site: http://www.iopl.org
The Institute of Political Leadership aims to guide the development of future leaders in areas of governance, ethics, and planning through the study and analysis of earlier leadership styles and interaction with other leaders.

Institute of World Politics
1521 16th Street NW
Washington, DC 20036
(202) 462-2101
Web site: http://www.info@iwp.edu
The Institute of World Leaders looks to develop an understanding of statecraft for developing leaders using knowledge of political systems, a grounding in ethical and social beliefs, and a commitment to peace.

Political Leadership Specialist Group
POLIS, University of Leeds
Social Sciences Building
Leeds, England
LS2 9JT
Tel: (0113) 343-4404
Web site: http://www.polis.leeds.ac.uk
Based in the University of Leeds, U.K., the Political Leadership Specialist Group looks at political leadership in western societies and analyzes them from different social, economic, ethical and theoretical perspectives.

FOR FURTHER READING

Arnold, James. *Saddam Hussein's Iraq*. Minneapolis, MN: Lerner Publishing Group, 2009.

Bhutto, Benazir. *Reconciliation*. New York, NY: HarperCollins Publishers, 2008.

Breen, Michael. *Kim Jong Il: North Korea's Dear Leader*. Singapore: John Wiley & Sons, 2012.

Gessen, Masha. *The Man Without a Face: The Unlikely Rise of Vladimir Putin*. New York, NY: Riverhead Books, 2012.

LaPoint, Ernie. *Sitting Bull: His Life and Legacy*. Layton, Utah: Gibbs Smith, 2009.

Mandela, Nelson. *Conversations with Myself: Nelson Mandela*. New York, NY: Farrar, Straus and Giroux, 2010.

Potter, Lawrence. *This May Help You Understand the World: From Bush's Blunderings to Global Glitches – the Problems of a Troubled World Made Easy*. London, England: Penguin Books, 2011.

Sabato, Larry J., ed. *Barack Obama and the New America*. Lanham, MD: Rowman & Littlefield Publishers, Inc, 2013.

Sullivan, Kimberley L. *Muammar Al-Qaddafi's Libya*. Minneapolis, MN: Twenty-First Century Books, 2009.

Zinn, Howard, and Rebecca Stefoff. *A Young People's History of the United States: Columbus to the War on Terror*. New York, NY: Seven Stories Press, 2009.

INDEX